Overcoming the Fear of Self-Promotion

Promote Yourself with Confidence as a Self-Employed Professional

C.J. Hayden

Wings for Business
Philadelphia, PA

The content of this book is for informational purposes only and is not intended to diagnose, treat, cure, or prevent any condition. You understand that this book is not intended as a substitute for consultation with a licensed practitioner. The author and publisher make no guarantees concerning the level of success you may experience by following the strategies described in this book, and you accept the risk that results will differ for each individual.

The author and publisher shall have neither liability nor responsibility to any person or entity with respect to any loss or damage caused, or alleged to have been caused, directly or indirectly, by the information contained herein.

If you do not wish to be bound by the above, you may return this book to the publisher for a full refund.

Overcoming the Fear of Self-Promotion
Promote Yourself with Confidence as a Self-Employed Professional
Copyright © 2022 C.J. Hayden

All rights reserved. No part of this book may be reproduced, stored in a retrieval system, or transmitted in whole or in part, in any form or by any means, electronic, mechanical, photocopying, recording, or otherwise, without written permission from the author or publisher, except for the inclusion of brief quotations in a review.

Published by Wings for Business
1500 Chestnut St, Ste 2 #1279 • Philadelphia, PA 19102
www.cjhayden.com

ISBN: 978-0-9855755-9-5

Contents

What to Know Before You Begin...1

One: You Can Learn to Manage Fear 5

Two: Building Your Fear-Defeating Muscles...............17

Three: Taming Your Inner Critic......................................29

Four: Identifying Your Self-Promotion Fears...............43

Five: Finding Your Personal Fear Antidote...................55

Six: Developing Your Fear Antidote 67

Seven: Quick Fixes for Fearful Moments.......................81

Eight: Defeating Fear with Stronger Relationships.....95

What to Do When You Finish this Book 107

Appendix 111

What to Know Before You Begin

Who will benefit from this book

Overcoming the Fear of Self-Promotion was written specifically for self-employed professionals and creatives—that valiant group of service providers who must market and sell their own services.

Some of the many self-employed pros who will benefit are: accountants, architects, attorneys, bodyworkers, brokers of insurance or real estate, coaches, consultants, counselors, designers, engineers, financial advisors, freelancers, health practitioners, IT specialists, photographers, speakers, therapists, trainers, and writers.

If you don't fit into any of those categories—perhaps you own a business that sells products, you're a jobseeker or student, or you're an employee with no sales responsibilities—you may still find many of the techniques in this book helpful to conquer your self-promotion fears.

For coaches, counselors, and other pros who help clients and students work through fear and resistance around self-promotion, you'll discover numerous approaches here that will aid you in supporting others. If you'd like expert assistance to coach, teach, or lead a group using this book's techniques, please see my companion book, the *Facilitator's Guide to Overcoming the Fear of Self-Promotion*.

Where this book came from

In the early 1990s, I began helping self-employed professionals get better at marketing and selling. Since then, I've coached and taught thousands of these folks. The first solution I came up with for them—for you—was my program *Get Clients Now!*™, which in 1999, first became a book.

With the *Get Clients Now!* system, my clients, students, and readers had in their hands the essential tools and structure they needed to create a simple, achievable, repeatable sales and marketing plan. The book has since been reissued in a second and then third edition, and sold over 120,000 copies.

But when it comes to marketing and sales, knowing what to do and how to do it isn't always enough. With no boss looking over your shoulder, you must constantly convince *yourself* to take steps that may bring up fear, resistance, and the voice of your inner critic.

That's why I developed my course "Overcoming the Fear of Self-Promotion," which has since been road-tested with hundreds of students. Many years of delivering this material as a multi-part workshop has enabled me to incorporate feedback from participants and keep making it better. Now I'm bringing the course to you in the form of this book.

Throughout the book, you'll read the words of students who have taken the course, sharing their experiences and insights about learning to manage fear. These lightly-edited dialogues will help you realize how universal your concerns about self-promotion may be, and see how others have applied what you'll be learning.

How to use this book

In eight chapters, each one sharing specific skills and ending with a skills practice exercise, you will learn:

- Where fear and resistance to sales and marketing comes from
- The seven most common fears of self-promotion
- How to identify when fear, resistance, and your inner critic are running the show
- What you can do to reprogram your thinking about promoting your business
- Special techniques you can use to promote yourself even when it scares you

I encourage you to go beyond just reading about these skills. Commit from the outset to complete the skills practice exercises that conclude each chapter, before reading further. By practicing the techniques you'll be learning, you will begin to integrate them into your way of thinking and acting. It's that practice that will give you the boost you need to conquer the saboteurs getting in the way of your business success.

When you finish this book, you will have absorbed a solid collection of tools and techniques to overcome fear and resistance around sales and marketing. And, if you also complete the included skills practice exercises, you'll have made substantial, experiential progress toward loosening the grip of those fears, and be on your way to becoming a more courageous marketer.

One: You Can Learn to Manage Fear

Confident self-promoters are made, not born

The majority of self-employed professionals and creatives who are good at marketing and selling didn't start out that way. When you see a businessperson who seems to do well at self-promotion, most of the time, that person has worked at it. The skills you need to successfully promote yourself and your business are skills you can learn—if you're willing to invest some time and effort.

Whether the part of sales and marketing that you find anxiety-provoking is making follow-up calls, or going to networking events, or becoming more visible online, or pitching your business to a panel of decision-makers, or all those things, you can learn how to promote yourself confidently.

Avoiding self-promotion is one of the primary factors that holds back self-employed pros from sales and marketing, and therefore, from having successful businesses. Sometimes you may experience your avoidance as fear, sometimes as resistance, or sometimes as procrastination.

For example, a task appears on your to-do list day after day, like "call Jane Spencer," and you eventually notice that, although other items on your to-do list are getting done, you are not calling Jane Spencer!

Sometimes you may experience this feeling as dislike or distaste—simply not wanting to market or sell because you find it unappealing or even repulsive.

I'll be talking about all the issues above in this book.

My personal journey with fear

Let me begin by sharing with you some of my own early experience with fear and how to walk through it. Even if you know me from some of my other work, this may be something that you've never heard about me before.

When I was 15 years old, I dropped out of high school, ran away from home, and never went back. Now, no child does that if things are great at home, but the part of my story I'm about to tell you is what happened *after* I left.

When I got out on my own, I had no money and very little education. There was no one I knew who was in a better place than I was. For months, I lived on the street and in shelters; I camped in the woods and on the beach; I slept on rooftops, in abandoned houses, and in a van that didn't run.

Every day of that time, I had to figure out how to eat and where to sleep. I panhandled for spare change, collected empty bottles for the deposits, lined up to eat in soup kitchens... all those things we see homeless people do in our cities today.

Eventually, I found work, rented a room, put myself thru school, and started to make a life for myself. But it took a long time, and none of it was easy. You can read more of my personal story in my memoir *Alias Rabbit*.

Once I got off the street, when I would tell people some of my history, they would say to me, "Wow, you must have had a lot of courage." But the fact is, I was terrified the whole time.

That's what I learned about fear that now I try to teach other people. Courage is not the absence of fear; it's the ability to take action while feeling afraid. You can feel afraid and still move forward; you can feel resistant and still do what it is that you're resisting.

I learned how to make my way in this big, scary world by learning how to *manage* my fear, and that's what I think you can learn to do, too.

You are not the only one who feels afraid

It's not just you who has some fear about marketing yourself. Throughout this book, I use the word "fear" as a blanket term for feelings that might show up as resistance, or take the form of a conversation with your inner critic, or of thinking you're a fraud or an imposter, or manifest as procrastination about sales and marketing. You are far from alone in struggling with these feelings.

Even today, when I have a thriving business and teach others how to promote themselves, I still experience fear and resistance about sales and marketing. If I need to pick up the phone and place a follow-up call, I still have that moment of worrying: "What are they going to say? How is this going to go?" But I've learned how to move forward and make the call anyway.

Self-employed folks don't tend to talk about this at Chamber of Commerce mixers, but almost everyone I've ever spoken with about this topic has admitted to some level of fear or reluctance about marketing and selling, regardless of how it may look on the outside. And, regardless of how successful they are!

The people who succeed at marketing and sales may not have ever eliminated their fear, but they have learned to manage it, so that it no longer matters whether or not the fear is present. That's exactly what this book is going to teach you to do.

Learning to manage your fear of self-promotion is a real possibility, not a pipe dream. One of my coaching clients was an attorney, and she wanted to transition from working for a large law firm to having her own mediation practice. But, she was fearful about promoting herself. As a lawyer inside a large firm, she was fairly anonymous. Other than a brief bio of her on the firm's website, there was little that the wider world knew about her.

But with her own business, she'd need a website that talked about not only her education and experience—the facts of who she was— but also her capabilities, her philosophy, and her way of doing things. Her fear was that people would read this information and be critical or skeptical of her. They would disapprove of what she was doing.

Because of this, she was afraid to let prospective clients or possible referral sources, and even her colleagues in law, learn what and how she thought. So, she was blocked from even getting started with her mediation business because she was afraid to launch a website.

We spent time working together on her fears using some of the techniques this book will share with you. As a result, she was able to get her website launched, and start networking to get clients.

Once she did this, she was pleasantly surprised to discover that there were colleagues who wanted to refer clients to her, and then people who wanted to hire her. This positive experience went a long way toward making her fear less significant. The fear didn't go away; she just stopped letting it stop her.

That's the mindset you need to have about fear of self-promotion. Maybe you'll never be able to make your fear vanish. But what you *can* do is stop letting it sabotage you.

When you promote your business, you're promoting yourself

When I first started working with self-employed pros to help them improve their marketing, I thought my clients and students just needed to know what to do. But then I discovered that even once they knew what to do, very often, they weren't doing it.

Sometimes, I could help them become more proactive about promoting their businesses by teaching time management techniques, or providing accountability, or coaching them in goal-setting and prioritization. But all too often, something else got in the way. They found themselves experiencing fear, resistance, or procrastination that had been triggered by deeper emotions.

Even people who were previously successful at marketing and sales—when they worked for an employer and promoted their employer's products and services—often faced unexpected challenges when they first started trying to promote their own enterprise.

Here's what was tripping them up.

Self-promotion has a special aspect for people like you who market their own services. When you promote your business, you are actually promoting yourself—*you* become the product. So, every time you try to get a client, engage a referral source, or land a contract, you expose yourself on a personal level to the possibility of rejection, disapproval, or failure.

When a prospective client declines to do business with you or simply doesn't return your email or call, it can make you feel personally rejected—as if there is something wrong with you as a person. Intellectually, you may understand that the person who says no to you is just making a business decision. But emotionally, you may feel unwanted, abandoned, or even attacked.

Those negative feelings quite naturally provoke a considerable amount of fear and resistance, as well as destructive comments from your inner critic. And so, you find yourself avoiding taking actions that will expose you to this unpleasant emotional experience. This avoidance can happen even without you being consciously aware that it's going on.

If you can learn to become more aware of your feelings about self-promotion—and the action or inaction those feelings provoke — you'll be on the path to learning how to manage your fear and resistance.

Skill: Managing fear with the I AAM Technique

The first simple approach to managing your fear and resistance is what I call the I AAM Technique. "AAM"—pronounced just like the word "am"—has 2 "A"s to remind you that there are 3 steps to this technique:

1. I am **A**ware.
2. I **A**ccept.
3. I can **M**ove ahead.

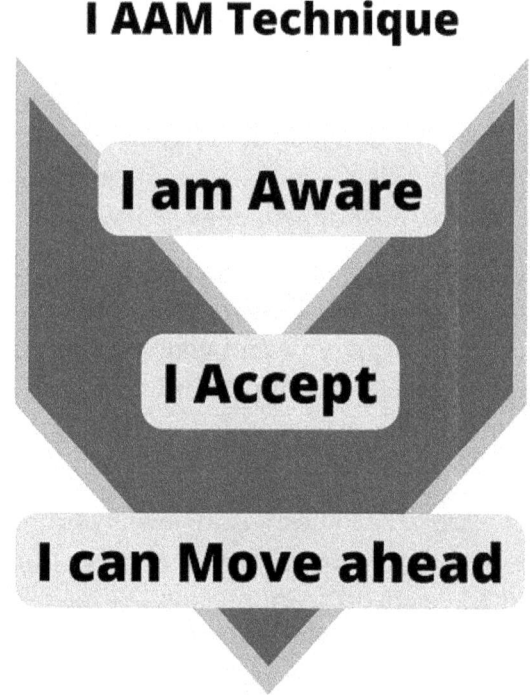

Here's how this technique works. When you notice that you're feeling afraid or resistant, realize that you can choose whether to let that feeling keep you from taking action. Then, choose that you will act.

1. I am Aware.

Begin by raising your awareness of what's happening. Say to yourself, "I'm aware that I'm afraid of making this phone call," or "I'm aware that I'm resisting going to that networking event," or "Wow, there's the fear again." This gives you an explanation for what's going on.

The way our minds work is that when we have an explanation for something, we have a much better chance of being able to manage it. All you're doing in this step is becoming aware of what is. You're not forming any judgments about it. There's no place in this step for beating yourself up about what you feel or think. Treat yourself with compassion.

Creating compassionate awareness of whatever is going on is the first step.

2. I Accept.

Next, tell yourself, "I accept that I'm afraid." Or, "I accept that I'm feeling resistant." Name what you're aware of and declare that you accept it.

Perhaps in the past, you denied that those feelings existed, or pretended they weren't present. With awareness, you're no longer denying or pretending. With acceptance, you're not trying to push past the feelings. Instead, you are acknowledging that they exist, and allowing them to be present.

3. I can Move ahead.

Once you have become aware of how you feel, and have accepted that you feel that way, you can then to choose to move ahead, despite how you feel. Say, "I am able to make this call anyway." Or, "I can go to that event even though I'm feeling resistant right now."

Declare your choice to move ahead whether or not you fully believe it. Notice that I'm *not* suggesting you should say you will move ahead without feeling any fear or resistance. It's perfectly okay to still be experiencing those feelings as you state your intention. All you need to do at this point is simply assert that you are choosing to take an action that is causing some fear.

You can make the three statements above out loud, or you can write them down. You might want to try both those approaches and see which one works better for you.

Why the I AAM Technique works

The three steps of the I AAM Technique—become aware of your sabotaging feelings, accept that they are there, and choose to move ahead anyway—form a simple, but very effective approach to begin working with your fear. It may seem like this is too simple to have much impact, but that's not so.

> Eckhart Tolle, author of *The Power of Now*, said:
>
> *"Once you see what you are doing... that unconscious pattern then comes to an end... Awareness is the greatest agent for change."*

You're probably already familiar with this phenomenon. Perhaps you've had the experience of going on a diet and having to record everything you eat. The simple act of writing down what you're eating—the writing, all by itself—will often change the way in which you eat. Instead of eating mindlessly, you bring your eating into consciousness by recording it. You make yourself more aware of what you're doing, in a non-judgmental, compassionate way.

Self-awareness, along with the skills of reflection and strategic thinking, are what researchers call metacognitive skills, the skills that make the most impact on learning and change. According to a Cornell University study of executives at top companies, the strongest predictor of their overall success was a high self-awareness score.

The inner conversation that we're having with ourselves when we take steps around sales and marketing can be constant. We think things like: "That sounded stupid; she must think I'm an idiot," or "I've got to get this perfect before I let anyone see it," or "I feel like a fraud when I say that," or "They probably don't think I'm good enough."

Most of the time, we try to ignore these thoughts, or push past them. But the conversation is still there. It makes us hesitant, or even avoidant; it slows down our reactions and response time. So, the point of developing your awareness is to make this internal conversation conscious.

Here's an example of how this might work. Let's say I'm sitting at my computer, and I've just written and reviewed a blog post. I notice that when it comes time to click the "publish" button, I'm hesitating. In the past, I may not have been conscious of what I was feeling, and told myself, "Let me just get another cup of coffee, and I'll review it one more time."

But then, I'd get distracted by something else, and never get back to publishing the post. The feeling I was having was uncomfortable, so I pushed it out of my mind. Now that I've learned the I AAM Technique, what I would do instead is tell myself, "Ah hah! I'm hesitating to publish this post because I have some fear around it."

Instead of pushing those feelings away, I would stop and examine them. I'd sit with the fear for a moment, then I would say aloud, "I'm aware that I'm afraid of what people will think of my writing. I accept that I have this fear. I can move ahead and publish this post even though this fear is present."

It's very likely that I would then feel able to click that publish button, because I've made myself aware of my fear, and made a conscious decision on what to do about it.

You may be thinking at this point something like this:

David: *It's really counter-intuitive. When the fear comes up, I feel some instinctual reaction to avoid it or overcome it. It feels like a very conscious effort to be with it.*

C.J: *That's right; it is counter-intuitive. It's a place where we have to retrain ourselves. When the fear comes up, instead of running away from it, to go through that process of awareness and acceptance. To say: "Oh, here's the fear. Okay, what is it that I'm afraid of? I'm afraid of failure. Got it."*

And, getting really conscious about the fact that this is exactly what's going on, instead of either trying to push it away, or push through it, which is the other kind of push we do. We say, "Okay, I'm not going to pay attention to that. Bye!"

David: *I also get that it's bringing it into focus—being more clear. What really is it? It's not just this gray mist of fear.*

When you understand what's happening, you can change it

The I AAM Technique enables you to raise your awareness of what's going on so you can shift it. By acknowledging, "I'm aware that I'm afraid," it makes it possible to accept that this is what's so—"I am afraid." Once you've done that, you now have the possibility of changing how you react to it. The process of learning to manage your fear requires you to first become aware that you have these fears to begin with.

I gave a class of self-employed professionals the assignment to compose a 10-second introduction, a 30-second commercial, or an elevator speech, then say it out loud to someone.

At the next class, here's what some of them said:

Peggy: *I noticed that my big fear was that people would "know" it was a commercial and be suspicious, and that I sounded phony.*

C.J: *You were afraid you sounded phony and that people would be suspicious. What else?*

Denise: *Every step of the way, my critic was just screaming loud and clear, "You don't even know who you work with." You know, the target audience. I was rebutted at every question. "You've got nothing to offer. You're not prepared." You know?*

C.J: *Your inner critic is very argumentative, Denise.*

Denise: *Very hard on me, yeah.*

C.J: *What other kinds of messages did people notice?*

Rick: *I guess my fear is like the more authentically I communicate who I am, the scarier it is. It's like I'm exposing myself at a more inner core, and all my insecurities just come raging out. The more I go authentic, the scarier it gets.*

C.J: *So that very authentic commercial that people liked, Rick, is probably the one that's the hardest for you.*

Rick: *Right, I mean I just have a big gulp in my throat even thinking about it.*

C.J: *It reveals the most, and that is the scariest.*

Rick: *Right.*

Skills practice: Try the I AAM Technique

Here's your first skills practice exercise. Try on the I AAM Technique, as I've described it in this chapter. The next time you notice that you are putting off some element of marketing or sales, that you are avoiding it, resisting it, or otherwise not getting it done, stop right there—in the moment that you notice it—and become a fear detective.

Ask yourself, "What's going on with me around this thing?" Consider it for a minute or two, then say out loud, or write down, or both: "I am aware that..." whatever feelings you are experiencing. Then, I accept that I am..." whatever you are feeling, and "I can move ahead with..." whatever you are avoiding or resisting, regardless of how you feel. Then see if you are indeed able to move ahead.

Try to take these steps without judging yourself. What you're experiencing is not wrong or bad, it simply *is*.

I suggest that you try using the I AAM Technique for two to three days before moving on to Chapter Two.

> Billie Jean King, the American women's tennis champion, once said:
>
> *"I think self-awareness is probably the most important thing towards being a champion."*

When you become more aware of your fear and resistance, you'll have taken a powerful step toward managing your fear.

Two: Building Your Fear-Defeating Muscles

What's going on in your head?

In Chapter One, you learned the I AAM Technique—to become aware of your sabotaging feelings, accept that they are there, and choose to move ahead anyway. Hopefully, you've had a chance to try out that technique and note some of the negative thoughts that come up for you when you market yourself. Or sometimes, when you even think about marketing yourself.

Here's what some self-employed professionals and creatives like you discovered, when they started noticing what was going on in their heads as they began to promote themselves.

> Rick: *The message that my brain is saying is: "Well, you don't really have anything to offer anyway, and nobody would really want anything that you have. So, just hide."*
>
> Judy: *I went through a whole big inner critic thing when we wrote our commercial: "I don't have anything. What am I faking here? What can I say?" To articulate them is just scary.*
>
> Vaughan: *My reputation will be ruined and I'll wind up homeless and starving, I mean that's what comes up for me.*

Noticing what you're thinking and feeling about self-promotion—like the folks above did—may have started to make you feel bad about yourself. Don't let it.

There's no reason to beat yourself up for having fears about marketing. Your upbringing and past experiences made you how you are. These are the cards you've been dealt. It doesn't help to make yourself wrong for it and think you shouldn't be that way.

Adding a burden of guilt or shame to how you feel isn't going to help the situation.

Accept that you are the way that you are. Accept how you're made, then get curious about it. How can you take who you are and make that work for you?

Lean on your strengths to overcome fear

One of my coaching clients hated going to networking mixers because she thought she was no good at small talk. It felt like a waste of time to go to those meetings and struggle to chat with people. But something she *was* skilled at was asking questions.

She had a background as a journalist and had conducted many fact-finding interviews. I suggested to her that she lean on that strength when attending an event. Instead of trying to force herself to talk about trivial subjects that didn't interest her, like the weather or traffic, she could make it her mission to interview the people she met to find out more about them.

The first time she tried this approach at a networking event, she relayed to me that she found herself completely comfortable meeting new people when she was wearing her reporter's hat.

By giving herself permission to employ the who, what, when, where, and why questions of journalism which she knew so well, she was able to bypass her dislike of small talk, and overcome her fears about attending events filled with strangers.

Skill: Learning new habits with the Practice Loop

The next skill for you to acquire is a technique designed for learning how to do anything new or challenging that might invoke fear or resistance for you. I call this approach the Practice Loop. The three steps of this technique are:

1. Prepare.
2. Practice.
3. Debrief.

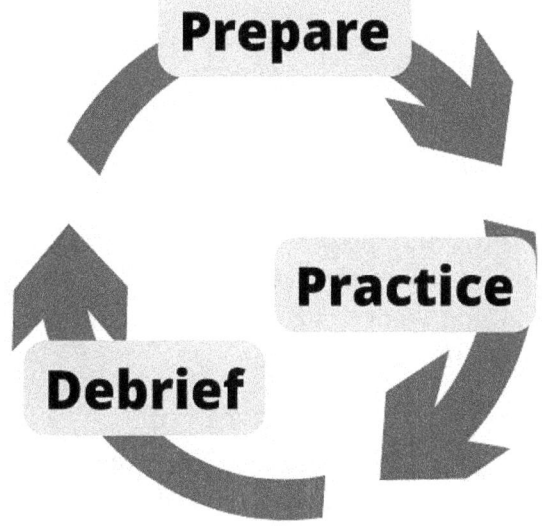

Here's how you use it.

1. Prepare. Decide to do something self-promotional that you find challenging. Prepare what you're going to say or do. Then, set an intention for how you're going to *be* while you're doing it.

Let's say you're about to attend a networking meeting, and you know you'll have to introduce yourself to people. So, you prepare by coming up with a 10-second introduction of yourself to use at the meeting. Your intention is that you will use your introduction with confidence.

2. Practice. Practice what you prepared to say or do. Your first practice might be in a safe environment. You could practice by yourself, perhaps with a mirror, or record yourself on audio, or take a video. Or, you could practice with your spouse, or a friend, or a business buddy. Or maybe you have a coach or a support group you could practice with.

After that first practice, you might try practicing out in the world: at a networking event, a coffee or lunch meeting, or in an actual sales conversation with a prospective client. You practice by saying or doing what you prepared, holding the intention for how to *be* that you decided on.

3. Debrief. After you practice, you debrief how your practice went. You ask yourself questions like:
- What worked about what you did, what you said, or how you were?
- What didn't work about it?
- What did you notice about what you thought, felt emotionally, or felt physically?
- What do you want to do or say differently, or how do you want to be different next time?

After completing all three steps, you repeat them, incorporating what you discovered when you debriefed. That's why this technique is called the Practice *Loop*. You keep repeating it, learning and adapting each time.

Putting the Practice Loop to work

The following dialogue shows more about how this technique works. The introduction shared by the student is real, but the student's last name and business name have been deleted.

C.J: *Nancy, thanks for being our volunteer. You had a moment to prepare. So, give us your 10-second commercial.*

Nancy: *It's funny, because I just was working on a new one today. I don't know if I should use my old one...*

C.J: *Use the new one; try it out on us.*

Nancy: *Alright. Hi, my name is Nancy [deleted]. My business is called [deleted]. What ideas are floating around in your head are your business. How you manifest them are my business.*

C.J: *Wonderful. I'm going to focus on just one piece of the debrief for this example. Nancy, what did you notice? While giving us your commercial, what did you notice that you were afraid of, or resisting, or that your inner critic had to say about it?*

Nancy: *I felt stupid, like I was saying lines in a school play.*

C.J: *Okay, you felt stupid. The inner critic said, "Oh, you're just saying lines here." So there was some stuff going on emotionally—feeling stupid. Your head was having a conversation with you. What about your body? Did you notice anything there?*

Nancy: *Yeah, I just shrunk down. Especially since it was something I haven't said out loud to anybody before, I kind of felt silly. I do feel like it's something canned. I'm not doing it in the natural course of conversation.*

C.J: *Yeah, there's all this commentary going on. That's the kind of stuff that's always there in the background as we're doing anything to promote ourselves. Our inner critic has stuff to say about it, we feel fear about what might happen, we resist activities that are going to make us feel uncomfortable. Given*

Two: Building Your Fear-Defeating Muscles

what you just noticed, Nancy, how would you manage that better next time?

Nancy: *I think it's a matter of practicing saying it out loud, and I think what you just said about the body language—to really stand up. Because most people really don't hear what you have to say. It goes in one ear and out the other. But they remember what you looked like when you were saying it, and how you were presenting yourself. That's something I think I became more aware of doing this exercise.*

C.J: *That's great information. How would you use knowing that?*

Nancy: *Next time—I have a networking meeting on Monday and we'll be doing introductions like that. I'll remember that when I'm there—just even when I'm walking into the room—not to shrink down.*

How to make the Practice Loop work for you

With the Practice Loop, you prepare, practice, debrief, and then loop around to take your learning into the next experience of doing a thing that you find scary. The more times you repeat this sequence, the more shift you will start to see.

What Nancy discovered was that her body shrank, and what might help her do better next time is to remember to stand up, stand straight, and hold herself as if she were somebody who wasn't afraid she was going to feel silly.

When you try the Practice Loop yourself, an essential component is to **notice what you notice**, then include that in your debrief. Ask yourself questions like these:

- What did you notice about what worked in what you said, did, or how you were? What did you notice didn't work about any of that?

- What did you notice going on with you in your head, heart, or body?
- What does your head say? Are you having thoughts like "who do you think you are" or remembering commandments like "don't brag"?
- What does your heart feel? Are you having reactions like "this is scary" or emotions like "I'm so nervous"?
- What does your body sense? Is your heart pounding or is your face flushed?

When you debrief after each practice, take careful note of everything you noticed about what happened. All change begins by starting where we already are. The more conscious you can get about what symptoms go along with fear for you, the more aware you become that it really is fear that's stopping you instead of some other cause. For example, sometimes fear masquerades as procrastination, or "not knowing how."

Admit what's going on in your head, heart, and body, without judgment or guilt. Be compassionate with yourself, and simply accept what's there.

After you've made note of all that you noticed, ask yourself:

- What do you want to do differently next time?

You might come up with a new thought you'd like to remember, or a feeling you'd like to try on, or a shift to how your body experienced what you did.

If you noticed that your head was saying "Who do you think you are?" you might tell yourself that next time, you'll silently respond with "I'm a skilled, talented professional, that's who."

If you realized that you were feeling insecure, you might decide that next time you'll take along a friend to stand beside you.

If you found yourself short of breath, you might remind yourself that next time you want to take three deep breaths first.

Two: Building Your Fear-Defeating Muscles

Whatever you notice about what's going on in your head, heart, and body, see if you can come up with one small thing to try next time to discover if it makes a difference.

The reason the Practice Loop technique works is because it creates a feedback circuit. Too often in marketing and sales, we engage in activities where we don't have any sort of feedback that helps us improve.

A feedback circuit like this gives you practical, real-time information about what works and doesn't work for you, which gives you the opportunity to try a different approach. It nudges you in the direction of more effective action. The Practice Loop works to help reduce fear and resistance because it helps you discover what specific words, thoughts, or actions make you, personally, feel less fearful.

In the dialogue with Nancy and her 10-second intro, I didn't tell Nancy what to do in order to feel less nervous about delivering her self-introduction. I asked her what she noticed about the experience, and what might help her change it for the better the next time she tried it. That way the answers are coming from you, instead of having someone else try to tell you what you should do.

According to James Clear, founder of The Habits Academy:

"Feedback loops are the invisible forces that shape human behavior."

Fear can hide behind resistance, procrastination, and avoidance

Sometimes the very act of debriefing after your practice can be a challenge, as you'll see in this dialogue.

> David: *As we do this, I realize that my cringe place is on the debrief. I sort of want to forget it and go on to the next thing. I'm willing to go out there to prepare and to do it, but then there's some piece that's challenging for me around actually thinking about it—like if it wasn't perfect, I'll be terrible or something.*
>
> C.J: *David, what might happen if you did the debrief?*
>
> David: *(Laughs.) I'd get some information.*
>
> C.J: *So that's a positive thing about what might happen, right? There might be some good, new, valuable information?*
>
> David: *Well, I'd have to admit I wasn't perfect, that it wasn't as good as it could be.*
>
> C.J: *That's what kicks up when you think about doing the debrief. In fact, it's probably even less conscious than that. What kicks in immediately is this thought "Well, yeah, but I might discover that I was doing it badly or not sounding right"—all of those possibilities.*
>
> David: *Then I'd be really embarrassed.*
>
> C.J: *Yeah, exactly. Notice how subtle this can be. The fear sometimes kicks in before we even realize that it's there.*
>
> David: *Uh huh, yeah.*

For many of us, whenever we have to promote ourselves, some form of fear comes up. Whether you're calling strangers on the phone, or writing copy for your website, or explaining why someone should hire you instead of a competitor, it's natural to experience a certain level of fear.

Sometimes we notice this as resistance rather than actually feeling afraid, and that resistance can often manifest as avoidance, like David described above, or as procrastination. If you find yourself writing something like, "Register for the next networking lunch" on your to-do list over and over and somehow it just doesn't get done, it's a good assumption that there's some fear at work.

Think of resistance, procrastination, and avoidance as hidden forms of fear, which means you can use the same fear-management techniques you are learning—the I AAM Technique and the Practice Loop—to help manage them.

Skills practice: Make use of the Practice Loop

This chapter's skills practice exercise is to try out the Practice Loop for yourself. You could apply this technique to any type of self-promotion activity, but I'm going to recommend you use a self-introduction, like Nancy used in my dialogue with her earlier in this chapter.

Prepare a 10-second self-introduction, practice it with another person or group of people, then debrief how it went. Remember while you're practicing to **notice what you notice**.

In the beginning, you may feel as if you're just stumbling around, and if you do, that's okay. This is how we learn to walk. We take a step, we stumble, we right ourselves, and we take another step. Stumbling is not bad or wrong; it's our learning process.

You may already have a 10-second self-introduction you like, and if so, it's just fine to use the one you have. If you need to create one, though, refer to "Crafting a Self-Introduction That Gets Noticed" in the Appendix for a guide that will walk you through how to do it.

To see how the Practice Loop can help you overcome fear and resistance, I recommend that you go through the loop three times with your self-introduction. Each time, prepare your introduction; practice it with a friend, a colleague, or a group; then debrief how it went and what you might try next time to make it less scary or difficult.

Use what you learn from your first debrief to revise your intro or change how you deliver it, practice it again with someone else, and debrief again. Then use your learning from the second debrief to prepare a third time, practice a third time with a different person or group, and debrief a third time.

Try it out at least one of those three times in a real world situation—like at a networking meeting, or with a potential client, or a possible referral source. Yes, that is scary, and that's the point. You're going to do something that makes your fear show up so that you can learn how to manage it.

When you begin thinking about using your introduction out in the world, you'll realize that you don't want to have to read it. So, you may need to take some time to memorize it first.

Notice that if you're thinking right now, "I won't be able to memorize it," or "I'm going to screw it up," that is your inner critic rising up and trying to get in your way.

Here's a trick to help you get past any struggles you might have with memorizing your intro, or with remembering it when you're feeling nervous.

> C.J: *Let me give you a different trick. Do you know the words to any songs?*
>
> Vaughn: *Um, yeah.*
>
> C.J: *Okay, I want you to think of a song that, to you, represents who you want to be about self-promotion. And then, put your commercial to that music in order to learn it.*

Rick: *How about "I'm too sexy for my..."*

(General laughter.)

C.J: *Perfect!*

Rick: *That would work!*

C.J: *Come up with a theme song. It's a mnemonic trick that works to help you memorize words, and it also will put you in the right frame of mind when you pick the right song. And nobody will ever have to know.*

If you do stumble while practicing your introduction, or when using it out in the world, remember that each time you practice, you're improving your skills for the next time. So long as you keep debriefing your practice, you will learn from it each time. Use the debrief questions I suggested in this chapter, or any others that you find helpful.

Remember that if at any point you find yourself feeling stopped by fear or resistance—feeling scared to try out your commercial, or feeling resistant, as David was, of doing the debrief—use the I AAM technique from Chapter One to help you move past any fear or resistance.

Seth Godin said:

"The best way to change long-term behavior is with short-term feedback."

Give the Practice Loop a try so you can experience that change for yourself.

Three: Taming Your Inner Critic

How your critical inner voice works

In Chapter Two, you learned how to use the Practice Loop to prepare for, practice, and debrief any self-promotion activity that provokes fear or resistance for you. I hope you were able to try out your self-introduction on others a total of three times, and that at least one of those times was in a real-world situation.

In your debriefs of delivering your self-intro, where I asked you to notice what you were noticing, it's a good bet that your inner critic made an appearance. Every one of us has some version of the inner critic: that voice in our heads that comments negatively on our abilities, compares us to others and finds us lacking, and makes us feel as if we aren't good enough at whatever we're doing.

Other names for this voice are "negative self-talk," "The Committee," or "The Gremlin," a label that was coined by Richard David Carson in his book *Taming Your Gremlin*.

Most researchers believe that where this voice comes from is the collection of messages you heard as a child, from parents, older siblings, teachers, clergy, or others who had an impact on how you see yourself. These childhood influencers may have given you what they thought was helpful advice, like: "Get good grades," or "Finish what you start," or "Stay safe."

Unfortunately, our childhood selves, eager to receive praise and approval from others, can internalize guidance like this in ways that ultimately have a negative impact.

"Get good grades" can become "You have to get an A+ at everything, or else you're not good enough."

"Finish what you start" can turn into "Keep trying harder even when you aren't sure you're on the right track. If you don't, you're a failure."

"Stay safe" can become "Don't take any risks, or bad things will happen to you."

Some of us also had imperfect influencers during our childhood years, who admonished us in ways that were negative to begin with. We may have been told, "You are always so sloppy," or, "What a lazybones you are," or, "Why can't you be smart like your brother?" Repeated critical messages like these turn into inner critic voices that tell us we are careless, lazy, or stupid.

Judgmental, disapproving commentary like this, coming from inside your own head, can play havoc with your ability to promote yourself successfully. It can make you hold back because you feel like you must be perfect, or keep stubbornly barking up the wrong tree because you don't want to be a loser, or avoid taking risks because you're worried you'll get hurt.

Allowing your inner critic to be the voice in charge of your marketing and selling carries a huge cost for you. It not only impacts your ability to promote yourself, but also your self-image, and even your overall sense of wellbeing. The good news is that—just like with fear—you can learn to manage your inner critic and take control of your thinking and actions.

How managing your inner critic improves self-promotion

Read this dialogue about what can happen once you learn how to manage your negative self-talk.

C.J: *What might shift about your sales and marketing?*

Woman: *It would be a lot more fun.*

C.J: *More fun? Yeah.*

Kenneth: *I know it would be more fun, but actually, I would be more present. More connected to the person, rather than thinking and wondering and strategizing in my head. I could actually be more present.*

Woman: *And they'll feel it.*

C.J: *And they'll feel it, that's right.*

Kenneth: *I wish I had heard this last week.*

C.J: *That's okay, you'll need it this week.*

Jim: *C.J., I think what I would say is I'll make more phone calls. There's some intention, some goals, some things I want to have happen, absolutely. But if I can let go of the outcome in the moment by being present, I'll make more phone calls, they'll be more fun, and it'll be much more authentic.*

C.J: *That is one of the things that happens. If you get more comfortable about what you're doing, you become more active. Because then you're not spending all that time with those mental gymnastics I referred to earlier, right? You're just doing the work, because you're not stuck in thinking, "Oh, what will happen if...?" We spend much more time doing that than I think a lot of us realize.*

Bob: *It strikes me that one of the reasons that we don't do more of the right things is that sometimes it's stressful. Because we're not comfortable. If we can become comfortable, that will show with our clients and they would rather work with someone who is comfortable than someone who is obviously stiff or not comfortable or uneasy.*

I guess it helps us two ways. One, if you're comfortable, you're likely to do more following up, and second, the client's more likely to want to talk to you, or be comfortable working with you.

C.J: *That's a really good point, because one of the things that happens for us as consultants is that the way we interact with the client when we're trying to sell them something is the only way they have to judge what it's going to be like to work with us as a consultant.*

The more we can be in our selling process like we actually are when we get into doing the work, the better we're going to be at landing clients that work for us and our style, and value what it is that we have to offer.

Skill: Disputing your inner critic

Here's a technique that can help you learn to manage your inner critic. It's a 3-step process:

1. Notice what the critic is saying.
2. Respond by disputing what the critic says.
3. Debrief the results and try it again.

This process is deceptively simple. But used over time, it can have dramatic results. Let's walk through it, step by step.

1. Notice what the critic is saying.

Don't try to just push through your uncomfortable feeling, or ignore that you don't feel good about what you're doing, or deny that the voice is there. Listen to what the voice has to say, and write it down.

You may wonder at times whether it's the voice of the inner critic you're hearing. Is it possible that instead this is your intuition speaking, or your internal wise advisor?

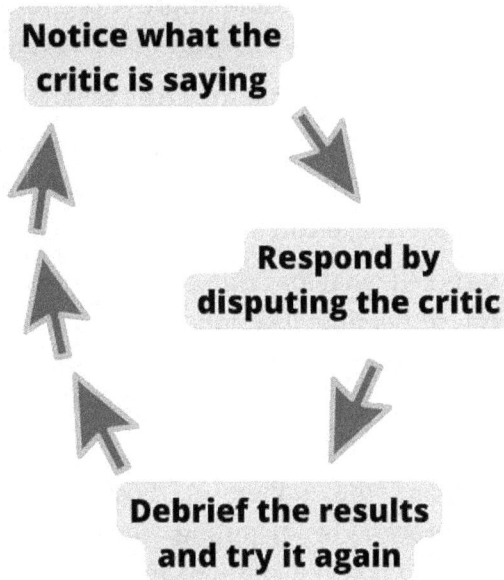

According to Tara Moore, the author of *Playing Big*:

The way that we can tell apart the inner critic voice in us from the voice of realistic thinking or positive critical thinking really has to do with the tone of the thoughts in our head... the inner critic will tend to be very repetitive and like a broken record, saying the same thing over again... It will be very black and white in its thinking... If it's talking to you in a way that is harsher and meaner than you would want to speak to someone you love, you're hearing the inner critic..."

For myself, I've noticed that while both the negative and positive voices in my head will make suggestions, my inner critic tends to deliver them as insults, while the positive voice in me, the wise counselor, invites me to step up and improve or grow. Listen closely, and you'll begin to know when it's your critic talking to you.

2. Respond by disputing what the critic says.

By noticing the negative thoughts of your inner voice, you're acknowledging that the critic is present. But that doesn't mean that you're allowing the critic to run the show.

When you've noted what the critic is saying, respond by disputing the message you're hearing. The inner critic is not telling you the objective truth. It's either outright lying to you, or it's misleading you by telling you something that may have been valid when you were a child, but no longer is.

Martin Seligman, the father of Positive Psychology, has researched this process of disputing negative self-talk and he recommends that you take one of three approaches:

- **Present evidence against what your critic is saying.** For example, if your critic tells you people will disapprove of you when you do anything to promote yourself, remind yourself of times that you got positive reactions to your marketing or sales efforts.
- **Give an alternative explanation for the critic's message.** For instance, when your negative self-talk suggests you'll never be able to make a sales call because you stumbled on the last one, point out that you hadn't practiced your talking points then, and now you have.
- **Question how useful that comment is.** E.g., if The Committee says you will forget your self-introduction when it's time to use it, respond by noticing how unhelpful that thought is, and resolve to instead focus on delivering your intro with confidence.

Disputing what your inner critic says has the impact of externalizing your internal conversation and bringing it out into the open where it can be dealt with.

3. Debrief the results and try it again.

After disputing your inner critic's message, debrief the results by asking yourself questions like these:

- How do you feel as a result of disputing your negative thoughts? Do you feel less fearful, less resistant, lighter, or more energized?
- Has the critic's message shifted as a result of your disputation? Does it seem less powerful, weaker, less truthful than before?
- What do you notice that worked about what you said, did, or how you were? What do you notice didn't work as well?
- What do you want to do differently next time?

Then try again to move forward on whatever the critic was interfering with.

How to work with the disputation steps

Here's an example of how these steps work. Suppose your critic says, "Don't ask that prospective client to hire you. He's going to say no." Your response is to notice that message from the critic and respond with a disputing statement.

You might **present evidence against the critic** by saying, "Well, he might say no, but I have no way of knowing that in advance. I need to ask to find out what he will say."

Or, you could **give an alternative explanation**, like, "Well, he could say no, but he could also say yes. Sometimes, people do say yes."

Or, you might simply **observe how that message isn't useful**, by saying, "It doesn't help me to focus on the possibility of hearing a no. If I allow that to stop me from asking, I'll never hear a yes."

Try one of those disputation options—whichever one seems the most helpful to you. Then notice how that thought makes you feel and whether the message is different now, or not as strong. Then try to move forward again. That one disputation might be enough.

If it isn't enough to get you moving forward, or if it works this time, but not the next time you try to ask for a sale, notice again what's going on. This time the critic might say, "You're not good enough to get a yes." And you again respond with a disputation.

You might **present evidence** like: "That's not so; I've gotten a yes at times in the past."

Or, an **alternative explanation**: "Maybe I'm not great at being a salesperson, but I'm really good at what I do. People who see that will want to work with me."

Or, **observe how that message isn't useful**. "There's no payoff in telling myself I'm not good at this. It defeats me before I start."

Then notice how that new disputation makes you feel, whether the message has shifted, and try to move forward once more.

Over time, as you work your way through disputing each comment that your critic makes, you will first of all, become more aware of this whole conversation going on in your head that is subconsciously preventing you from taking action.

And secondly, you will start to come up with a wide variety of ways to reassure the protective internal voice that wants to keep you from getting hurt. You'll be letting the critic know that you're okay on your own, that you know what you're doing, that you're capable of taking steps that scare you, and that these negative messages aren't helpful.

If you continue to do this, it will make your inner critic loosen its grip on you.

You may have already encountered the acronym where F.E.A.R. stands for False Evidence Appearing Real. Remembering this can be highly effective. Fear of self-promotion rarely represents the truth.

Once you learn to respond to fear with a truer statement, a statement of disputation, you can reduce its power over you.

How to get past a stubborn inner critic

What if you're working with the disputation skill, and it feels like you're making progress, but still, you sometimes feel immobilized by negative self-talk? Are there any tricks you can use that maybe won't fix this problem forever, but just get past your inner critic today, so you can do the marketing and sales you need to do?

Yes, there are. Read this dialogue.

> Suzanne: *I would rather put a stick in my eye than pick up the phone. Even with any networking connections, I just really hate to pick up the phone. But I know that it's a necessary evil. So, what are some tips, tricks that I might be able to try to get myself to not hate to pick up the phone so much. I mean, I really hate it.*
>
> C.J: *You're definitely not alone with that issue. It's something that's really, really common. It does seem to get easier if you have some sort of connection or relationship with the people you're calling, but sometimes, it is just the hardest thing to do. I find that for some people, even a connection or relationship doesn't always do the trick because sometimes you attach even more weight to it then.*
>
> Suzanne: *Exactly.*
>
> C.J: *In a situation like that, where you're feeling, "I know I need to do it, and I don't wanna do it," for me, the thing that has always worked is to trick myself. I've learned that even though I will procrastinate eternally about getting on the phone, when I actually do it, it's nowhere near as painful as I thought it was going to be, once I'm actually talking to somebody.*

Three: Taming Your Inner Critic

For me, what has really helped to get myself off the dime and take a step I'm not fond of is to do things that will put me into the right frame of mind to make that call. I'll give you some suggestions about what those things might be.

Standing up, instead of doing it sitting down. Or, looking either into the mirror at myself and smiling, or looking out the window at the world and getting a broader perspective instead of thinking about me and my little problems.

Another thing that has really worked for me is beginning my phone calls by calling someone I know to talk about something other than my business and selling something.

For example, calling up a friend, and having a very brief conversation with that friend, and then as soon as I'm done with that conversation, not even hanging up the phone. Just pressing the switchhook and dialing the next number while I'm still in that talking-to-my-friend frame of mind.

That's what I mean by tricks to get me off the dime. I usually find that if I can make that first call and get into conversation with someone, that will keep me going.

Suzanne: *I do have that on my list, but I still dread it. [Laughs.] It's a real challenge for me. And the other thing I run into also is that I get a lot of voice mail. And I actually look forward to getting a voice mail rather than a real person, which is horrible, horrible.*

C.J: *But yet, it's a fact. It's the way that you feel about it, and I'm with you completely.*

Skill: Tricks to get past your inner critic quickly

Here's a summary of the quick tricks I mentioned in the above dialogue with Suzanne. These can help you move past your inner critic, whether you're trying to get yourself on the phone, or write a marketing email, or work on copy for your website:

- Stand up instead of sitting down.
- Look in the mirror and smile.
- Look out the window and gain perspective on the wider world instead of being isolated with your personal problems.
- Talk to a friend before reaching out to a prospective client. This will often work even if you're just talking to your friend's voice mail.

Another tactic that can be useful to bypass your critical inner voice is to address it directly and take charge of the situation. For example, say, "Listen, buddy," or "Listen, missy, I can't stop you from being here, but you don't get to be the one making the decisions."

Some people find it helpful to assign their inner critic a name or visual image. This helps you to externalize the voice, and not accept it as your own. My name for my own inner critic is "The Schoolmarm." She wants everything done perfectly and insists I should work hard all the time.

It can be helpful to caricature your critic, so you can discount it or make fun of it. For example, you could give your critic the name Big Bad Wolf, so you could tell yourself, "Who's afraid of the Big Bad Wolf?" Or, picture your critic as the classroom teacher in *Peanuts* cartoons whose voice always sounds like, "Wah wah woh wah wah."

Three: Taming Your Inner Critic

Dr. Lisa Firestone, co-author of *Conquer Your Critical Inner Voice*, said:

"Remember not to act on the directives of your inner critic... by identifying, separating from, and acting against this destructive thought process, you will grow stronger, while your inner critic grows weaker."

If you use quick-fix tricks like these to empower yourself to move forward in the near term, and also keep working with the longer-term approach of using the disputation technique described above, over time, your relationship with your inner critic will shift.

The dialogue I began with Suzanne above continued like this:

> C.J: *I think for probably the first five years I was in business, I spent a lot of time thinking, "Do I really have to pick up the phone and call those people?"*
>
> *There was a moment when it started to shift for me, and I no longer had to use tricks to get myself into the right frame of mind and force myself to make a call. The moment when it shifted—I remember it vividly; it was that dramatic.*
>
> *I was sitting there looking at a long list of prospective clients, then looking at my not-empty, but not-quite-full appointment book, and thinking, I really, really, have to call them. But I was mired in inner critic conversations about how I wasn't a salesperson.*
>
> *All of a sudden, an alternative thought came to me in a flash, "You know, you could really help those people. You could make a difference in their lives and in their businesses, if only they would just agree to work with you. By sitting here not being willing to make those calls, you are depriving those people of*

your help. So, get off the dime, pick up the phone, and help some people."

It shifted my perspective in such a remarkable way that it never swung back again. I started thinking each time about what I could do for a potential client instead of thinking, "Oh, poor me, I need to make a sale."

Suzanne: I like that way of thinking. If I don't call them, I can't help them. I like that perspective.

Skills practice: Try out managing your inner critic with disputation and quick tricks

The next time your inner critic shows up around self-promotion, try the three-step disputation formula from this chapter, then debrief what happens. You'll get the most benefit if you try out the formula on three separate occasions before you move on to Chapter Four.

If you need to, also try some of the quick tricks I suggested to keep yourself moving forward right away.

>Elizabeth Gilbert, the bestselling author of *Eat, Pray, Love*, says she handles her inner critic by addressing it this way:
>
>*"Dearest Fear, Creativity and I are about to go on a road trip together. I understand you'll be joining us because you always do... You're allowed to have a seat, and you're allowed to have a voice, but you're not allowed to have a vote... above all else, my dear old familiar friend, you are absolutely forbidden to drive."*

Three: Taming Your Inner Critic

Keep remembering that you are not the only one struggling with a critical inner voice. A bestselling author like Elizabeth Gilbert has one, and a veteran at marketing and sales like myself has one.

We all have an inner critic. Some of us have simply learned to manage it better, and that's exactly what you are learning how to do.

Four: Identifying Your Self-Promotion Fears

Why you should get to know your fear

In the first three chapters, you learned that the best approach to overcoming fear, resistance, and your inner critic is not to deny these saboteurs exist, or try to make them go away, but instead, to discover how to manage them when they show up.

In this chapter, you'll learn how and why to explore in more depth some of the fears you might be experiencing. In the many years that I've been working with clients and students on building their businesses, I've identified seven distinct fears of self-promotion. Getting to know your fears better is an essential step in becoming able to manage them.

> According to sociology professor Christopher Bader, who conducted a fear survey for Chapman University:
>
> *"Sometimes when we're afraid of something, even if our fears are irrational, that can lead us to make choices that will actually cause the thing that we are avoiding."*

Here's an example of what Bader is referring to. One of my coaching clients was terrified of failing. Her overcritical parents had instilled in her the belief that if you failed at anything, it meant you were unworthy of love and attention.

Because she was so afraid of failure, she avoided taking on anything new that would require her to try something she didn't already know how to do well. By refusing to try any new techniques to market her business, she was causing her business to fail.

For example, she'd never tried developing referral relationships, even though she knew that in her profession, that was absolutely the best way to get clients. Because she'd never done it before, she was

Four: Identifying Your Self-Promotion Fears

afraid she would fail at it, and her fear of failing prevented her from trying it. Her fear was causing the very result she was afraid of.

Once you identify exactly what you fear, you have a point of reference for working to overcome it. Understanding precisely what you're afraid of provides you with a concrete issue to address. You must increase your conscious awareness of what's going on—acknowledge that indeed you are afraid—and specifically what you're afraid of.

The more awareness you have of what is operating within you, the more manageable it will ultimately become. In order to manage your fears, you have to know what they are. This means quite literally assigning them labels.

> The legendary Star Wars character Yoda said:
>
> *"Named must your fear be before banish it you can."*

Skill: Recognizing the Seven Fears of Self-Promotion

By listening to the struggles of many self-employed professionals and creatives, I've identified seven different fears of self-promotion. As I describe these seven distinct fears, think about which ones most likely apply to you.

1. Rejection. With fear of rejection, you're afraid that people won't want you. You think, "What if I ask for the sale, and the person I'm asking says no?" You don't like to feel unwanted, and that's how rejection makes you feel—like someone doesn't want you. Or sometimes, like no one at all wants you.

Fear of rejection is one of the most common reasons self-employed pros are reluctant to market or sell. If you're afraid of being rejected, you don't want to put yourself out there.

2. Ridicule. Fear of ridicule sounds like, "What if I try to introduce myself in front of a group, and people make fun of me?" It's hurtful when people make fun of you, so you're afraid of experiencing that.

Perhaps you're new in business and suffering from what some call the Imposter Syndrome, so you're afraid someone will say, "You're doing what now?"

3. Embarrassment. When you fear embarrassment, you're afraid that you'll forget what you were going to say at a speaking engagement, or that you'll get tongue-tied during a sales call, or that you'll trip and fall when you walk up to the buffet table at a networking lunch.

When you fear that you'll do something stupid or clumsy, you avoid taking any steps that might result in embarrassment.

4. The unknown. Fear of the unknown can become a serious obstacle. For example, if you feel like you don't know how to describe what you do in a sentence, you may hold back from introducing yourself. Or, if you think you don't know how to make a formal sales presentation, you may resist reaching out to a corporate client who you know will want that.

You're afraid of situations that might make you feel in over your head or out of your control. When you don't know what might happen, you're afraid of that.

5. Failure. When you practice catastrophic thinking, this is an expression of fearing failure. You imagine the worst possible result at all times. If you call someone, you visualize them hanging up on you, or see yourself saying something completely wrong. Or, you imagine that you'll put weeks of effort into pursuing a major sale and it will all be for nothing.

You fear that if you make an appointment for a networking conversation, when the time comes, you won't be able to go through with it. Since you're afraid you might fail, you become afraid to even try.

6. Success. At first, the idea of fearing success might seem a bit odd. But this fear is what can be at work when you carry your catastrophic thinking even further out into the future. You imagine that you will land a major contract, and then you won't be able to perform the work. Or that you will be so busy that you'll neglect your family. Or that your friends won't like you anymore because you're now too big and important.

You fear that if you become successful with your business, certain people will be jealous or resentful, or you'll feel guilty, or you'll have to deal with some other messy thing in your life that you've been avoiding. Or, you may feel a sense of entrapment—that you'll become trapped by your success; you'll have to be "on duty" all the time.

When you fear what might happen in the future, it can stop you cold in the present. When fear of success is operating in the background, you can sabotage yourself because a part of you doesn't want to succeed. You hold yourself back, thinking "I'd better not promote myself too much."

7. Disapproval. With fear of disapproval, you worry that if you become more visible promoting your business, if you expose yourself, people will disapprove, or withdraw their affection, or criticize you. Fearing that disapproval, you're afraid to show up, so you withdraw into your shell.

If you hold a belief that sales is manipulative, or marketing is sleazy, you may stop yourself from marketing and selling. You aren't comfortable with behaving like your negative image of a salesperson. Maybe you picture a used car salesman, manipulating or even cheating people. Or you imagine a pushy telemarketer who you can't get off the phone.

You don't want to be like those people, so you don't want to market or sell and have others think of you in that disapproving way.

Those are the seven specific fears that I've identified. My suggestion for starting to get a handle on managing them is to decide which one is usually the hardest for you. You may have them all at one time or another, but which one of the seven seems to give you the most trouble? Or is troubling you the most right now?

Allow yourself to name your fears without being bludgeoned by judgment or guilt. Don't berate yourself for being afraid. Remember that fear is a natural human reaction to feeling at risk, and that some level of fear of self-promotion is perfectly normal for self-employed professionals and creatives.

According to neuropsychologist and brain-training expert Theo Tsaousides:

"Feeling fear is neither abnormal nor a sign of weakness: The capacity to be afraid is part of normal brain function. In fact, a lack of fear may be a sign of serious brain damage."

Skill: Discovering your primary self-promotion fear

In the next lesson, we'll look more deeply at how to use the label you choose for your most challenging fear to help you better manage it. But first, you need to give it a name.

To identify which of the seven fears is the most challenging for you, think about a specific instance recently when fear, resistance, or the inner critic showed up while trying to promote your business.

Was it when composing an email to a prospective client? Calling a stranger on the phone? Talking to someone about your business who knows you well? Putting your thoughts in writing on your website or in a blog post? Going to a networking event? Standing up in front of a group to introduce yourself?

If you're still having trouble naming which fear gives you the most trouble, try stepping into it more fully. Picture the scariest marketing or sales scenario you can come up with. Then, let your imagination run wild. What could happen if you put yourself in that situation? If you made that move and what you feared came to pass, what would that awful event be? How does thinking about the possibility make you feel?

Rather than trying to figure it out with your mind, let your emotional reaction guide you. What comes up when you think about a frightening aspect of self-promotion? When you imagine the possible consequences, what feelings arise?

Sometimes it's hard to recognize a feeling just by pondering it in your brain. Try tapping into what your body is feeling. Are your neck muscles tensing? Are you holding your breath? Does your stomach feel queasy? When else has your body felt exactly that way? What fear was most likely operating at that other time?

If you're still not sure what label would best name your fear, here are four other avenues you might try:

1. Stream of consciousness journaling or free writing can often surface thoughts and feelings that you haven't been able to articulate previously. Set pen to paper, or your fingers to the keyboard, and write without stopping for ten minutes about what might be blocking you in self-promotion.

Whatever comes to mind, write it down. Don't stop to think about it. Don't lift your pen or typing fingers until the ten minutes are up. Then see what you have.

2. Try dream analysis, which can help to unearth feelings that are sitting below the conscious level. Just before you go to sleep at night, ask yourself a specific question about the area where you feel blocked. You might say, "Why am I stalling on following up with those leads?" or "What is so scary about attending a networking event?"

As soon you wake up, try to remember what you dreamed about, and describe it to yourself in as much detail as possible. What was the setting? What people or animals were present? What objects did you encounter? What actions did you take or were taken by others?

Dreams are sometimes quite literal, but more often use symbols to communicate with us. For each of the settings, characters, objects, or actions that appeared in your dream, ask yourself what it reminds you of in real life. If you're interested in exploring this powerful self-discovery technique further, an excellent resource is Gayle Delaney's book *Breakthrough Dreaming*.

3. Work with a business coach or life coach who can ask you powerful questions about your fears or inner critic conversations. Interacting with an impartial, compassionate thinking partner can draw out insights from within you that may not be as easily accessible when working on your own.

4. Express it in images instead of words. Draw, paint, or collage the negative thoughts you have about self-promotion. Once you've created a portrait of how you feel, put it aside for a day. Then look it over and try to name what you see in your visual representation.

Quite often, we're afraid of the idea or belief that our fear represents rather than the thing we might think is making us fearful. For example, when you start to look, you might discover that a fear of attending networking events is actually because you're concerned that you don't look "professional" enough. This fear isn't about the setting—it's not networking meetings that make you afraid. Instead, you might be fearing disapproval from the people you could meet there.

If you face your fear head on, examine it, and give it a label, you may immediately start seeing something to do about it. Once you drag a fear into the light, it stops being an invisible monster under your bed and turns into a problem you can realistically solve.

All seven of the self-promotion fears have certain things in common. Here's what a couple of my students noticed about them:

> Nancy: *They relate to self-worth.*
>
> C.J: *They sure do, don't they? They really are about self-worth, and that gives us an important clue to how we might be able to manage them. Anything else you notice about the seven fears?*
>
> Nancy: *They're really perceptions.*

C.J: *Great, Nancy, say more about that—that they're perceptions.*

Nancy: *They're perceptions that we have in our head. It's not necessarily the way that other people are viewing us. It's just in our heads.*

C.J: *That's a very important thing to keep in mind.*

Nancy: *It's that F.E.A.R. acronym; that's what it's all about— False Evidence Appearing Real.*

Trina: *I notice that it's all tied in with our self. To take that a little further, it's about not trusting ourselves, not being able to trust that we can handle whatever comes up for us, and being able to move through that.*

Realizations like these about what's going on when we experience self-promotion fears can be very helpful in setting us on the path to manage them.

When you notice that these fears are based on your own perceptions, that they are expressions of your sense of self-worth or of not trusting yourself, you begin to recognize that they are indeed "false evidence." They are not based on objective, current-day reality.

Skills practice: Practice self-promotion and identify your fear

Your skills practice for this chapter is to practice a form of self-promotion that you find scary, and identify the fear you experience.

For example, let's say you find yourself holding back on directly asking for business because it feels yucky to you. First, prepare. Write out some ways you could ask for business. Depending on the situation, you might say "Could we talk about the possibility of us working together?" or "Would you like to sign up?" or "Here's what I propose... How does that sound?"

Then, practice. The next time you find yourself in a situation where asking for business, or at least asking to have a sales conversation, would be appropriate, use one of the phrases that you prepared to make a direct ask.

Afterwards, debrief. Ask yourself these debriefing questions:

- What worked about what you did, said, or how you were?
- What didn't work about it?
- What did you notice while you were doing it—in your head, in your heart, and in your body?
- What was it you were afraid of? Was it rejection, ridicule, embarrassment, the unknown, failure, success, or disapproval? It may feel like more than one, or maybe even all of them at times, but which one felt the strongest, or which one came up most often?

Make note of that fear to work with further in Chapter Four. If you're having trouble deciding, use one of the approaches I described earlier in this chapter to explore more deeply what you're experiencing.

If you're still having trouble deciding, just pick one fear to work on. You'll be able to practice the techniques you're about to learn by working with that fear, and later on, you can use those same techniques on any other fears that show up for you.

After you've made a note of which fear seemed the strongest for you, remember to ask the last question you should always ask when you debrief:

- What do you want to do differently next time—in your words, thoughts, or actions?

Be forewarned that thinking about your fears at this in-depth level can feel unpleasant. Here's what some other self-employed professionals said about this chapter's skills practice.

Rick: *Reading these just takes me into the pit.*

C.J: *Notice the yucky feeling that this creates!*

Rick: *It does.*

C.J: *This is why we avoid thinking about it.*

Rick: *Ooh!*

Denise: *Especially when you say yes to all of them.*

(General laughter.)

....

Eleanor Roosevelt said:

"You gain strength, courage, and confidence by every experience in which you really stop to look fear in the face."

....

That's what this skills practice exercise is designed to do for you.

Acknowledging that yes, this can be yucky stuff to deal with, here's the path that you're now on. If you can name the fears that you're struggling with, you can discover their antidote. You are learning how to manage your fear.

One of the positive results that practicing out in the world can create is to make what you're doing feel real. If you have any difficulties with the Imposter Syndrome, the experience of talking about your business to others—and having them take you seriously—can be a powerful remedy.

Four: Identifying Your Self-Promotion Fears

If you're eager to move on to the next chapter before you'll have a chance to practice self-promotion with anyone in real life, you can practice in a safe place instead—with a friend, colleague, or coach. But be sure you've chosen one specific fear to work with before you start the next chapter.

Five: Finding Your Personal Fear Antidote

What self-promotion fear did you notice?

In the last chapter, you learned how naming your fears about self-promotion can grant you power over them. The skills practice exercise for the chapter was to notice the fear, resistance, or inner critic chatter that came up for you while you were practicing promoting yourself, then identify which of the seven fears of self-promotion you found yourself experiencing the most strongly.

Here's what some other self-employed pros said about the process of identifying their fears.

> Denise: *I noticed for me that it was the "ridicule" one, because all the self-talk was about me ridiculing myself. So, I guess I tend to expect that from people, especially offering something like coaching, that's so different from what I currently do.*
>
> C.J: *Okay, so ridicule's the number one to work on. And, there may be others down there.*
>
> Denise: *Yeah, there's definitely all the others.*
>
> C.J: *Usually there's one or two that surface up at the top, and they're the place to begin.*
>
> Joyce: *Mine didn't fall into any of these seven categories.*
>
> C.J: *What did you come up with?*
>
> Joyce: *I don't know, maybe it's just another way of reacting. Every time, I'd think, "What if I get a lot of business; how am I going to ever manage it?" That was one fear. I don't think I can handle it, if this really works.*
>
> C.J: *May I categorize that one for you?*

Joyce: *Yeah.*

C.J: *It's fear of success.*

Joyce: *Fear of success?*

C.J: *Absolutely.*

Joyce: *And the other was of course, the Imposter Syndrome, like I mentioned before. What would that be under?*

C.J: *My categorization of that—and of course, all this is arbitrary—but in terms of a place to look, I'd put that one under disapproval. Because the fear is that if you're not who you say you are, if you're a faker, then people will disapprove. But your first fear: "If I do this, how am I going to handle it? Will I be stuck with it? Will I be able to handle it? Will I have to do it all the time? How can I sustain it?" All of that is part of fear of success.*

To manage your fear, make friends with it

In previous chapters, you explored raising your awareness of fear and resistance and accepting their presence without judgment. Now I'm going to invite you to go further than acceptance—to get into alliance with your fear. To actually make friends with it.

What we often do when we start to feel afraid is we try to fight it. We tell ourselves: "Oh no, I'm not afraid," or, "I'm not going to think about that." We deny it, or we avoid it. We delay doing anything about it. But fighting fear with denial and avoidance is like fighting fire with gasoline. The fear just gets stronger.

When you put energy into denying and avoiding fear, that energy reinforces those feelings.

Overcoming the Fear of Self-Promotion

Psychologist Carl Jung noted:

"What you resist not only persists, but will grow in size."

The more you try to push fear down, the more it flares up.

Fear is already part of our experience, so to change how we relate to it, we must start from where we are. Your fear is a part of yourself; how can it be good to fight it?

In reality, your fear is a defense mechanism. Your fear's job in your life is to prevent you from getting hurt. In the physical world, fear of heights may keep you from getting too close to the edge of a cliff.

In self-promotion territory, if you don't do the things you're afraid of, you won't be rejected, made fun of, or fail. So, your fear tries to stop you from doing those things.

If you fear rejection, you don't make follow-up calls, so no one says no to you, and you don't get hurt. If you fear disapproval, you don't take any steps to stand out, so no one notices you, and they can't disapprove. If you're afraid of success, you avoid promoting yourself so that it won't happen.

Of course, you also don't get any business if you avoid self-promotion, and that's the point of doing the work described in this book.

Every kind of fear that we have about promoting ourselves is the result of our minds and our emotions trying to keep us safe.

The true path to becoming able to manage your fears is to get into alliance with them, so you can reassure them. These feelings are going on within you; they're a part of you. Instead of trying to deny them or fight them, we need to make friends with our fears, find out what they need, and try to provide that.

Five: Finding Your Personal Fear Antidote

Now, I understand that what I'm asking you to do is counter-intuitive. I'm asking you to break what may be a lifelong habit of "whistling in the dark." In other words, you've been trying to conquer your fear by covering it up, or even by denying that you're afraid at all.

But here's what Sigmund Freud had to say about that:

"When the wayfarer whistles in the dark, he may be disavowing his timidity, but he does not see any the more clear for doing so."

When I suggest that you make friends with your fear, I'm proposing that—instead of covering up or denying fear—you go deeper into it to find out what it needs from you to loosen its grip. Then, work on developing strengths that could reassure your fear. You might think of this as creating a fear antidote.

For example, if you're afraid of rejection, what might reassure that fear? What antidote could make your fear of rejection believe that you no longer need its protection to keep from getting hurt? Well, if you worked to build your confidence, rejection could no longer hurt you. So, that fear would begin to lessen.

Instead of fighting your fear of rejection, the more powerful solution can be to work on building your confidence. By doing that, you're replacing negative impulses with positive thoughts and focused action.

Learning to control your reaction at the impulse level is essential because fear and resistance are emotional responses, not reasoned ones. They are triggered at the base of your brain, the province of your primal or reptilian brain, which tells you within a split-second after experiencing fear that you should have a fight, flight, or freeze response.

This emotional reaction happens so quickly that it's difficult to counter it with conscious thought. That's why you must literally retrain your brain to react differently.

Read this exchange I had with one of my students on this topic:

> TM: *There's something I read recently which makes so much sense, because a lot of our fear is our imagination. It says that when imagination and logic are in conflict, imagination will win. For example, I called somebody on their cell phone and on their business phone, and when they didn't answer, my imagination said they saw my number and didn't want to answer. Now is that logical? No. But my imagination made it up, and made it so.*
>
> C.J: *That's great, TM, and what it points up is how much stronger our emotions can be than our thinking. When we imagine something awful and have an emotional, visceral reaction to it, that prevents us from hearing what our conscious minds are thinking, even if our head is trying to tell us we're going to be okay. That's why I think it's so essential to try and reassure that fear at an emotional level, so that you're countering emotion with emotion instead of just countering emotion with thinking.*

This concept of making friends with your fear, and developing a positive antidote to it, isn't some crazy idea that I've cooked up on my own. Many experts agree with this approach to managing fear.

Five: Finding Your Personal Fear Antidote

For example, Dr. Denise Fournier of Nova Southeastern University said:

"...when we can extend compassionate kindness to the things we fear, aiming to accept them as they are, we make it possible for the fear to dissipate... A positive relationship with fear is not only possible—it's transformative."

Dr. Andrew Shatte, author of *The Resilience Factor*, said that the way to overcome fear and anxiety is to "build the positive," such as "optimism, hope, good emotions, meaning, and purpose."

Skill: Find your fear antidote

In the last chapter, I asked you to identify your most challenging fear. With that awareness, you can now define what antidote to that fear might work best. For each of the seven fears of self-promotion, there's a quality you can develop within yourself to reassure your fear.

1. Fear of rejection tries to make you believe that people won't accept or approve of you. It holds you back from reaching out to potential clients.

What this fear needs for reassurance is for you to develop the positive quality of **confidence**—confident people never feel rejected, because they're sure of their capabilities and of the value of what they're offering. If you're confident, rejection can't hurt you.

2. Fear of ridicule gets you to think that others are going to make fun of you. Whether you fear laughter, teasing, or even bullying, this fear can prevent you from doing anything to be noticed.

This fear needs **self-assurance**—if you're comfortable with who you are, then you don't perceive that people are laughing at you, instead you see that they're laughing *with* you when something silly happens.

3. Fear of embarrassment tries to convince you that your dignity or competence is at stake. You might fear you'll be seen as a "loser" or a "dummy."

This fear wants **comfort**. If you're comfortable with your surroundings, and feel at home with where you are and what you're doing, you don't get embarrassed. Instead, you feel like you belong where you are, and whatever you do will be okay.

4. Fear of the unknown sparks the imagining of consequences that may have no basis in reality. When we don't know what's going to happen, we may make up all sorts of negative possibilities.

This fear wants **knowledge**. You learn enough, or prepare enough, to eliminate more and more of the unknowns. The more knowledge or evidence you have, the fewer unknowns there are.

5. Fear of failure makes you avoid risky situations where you might fail and experience emotions like frustration, shame, disappointment, sadness, regret, or even anger.

What this fear needs is a **belief in the possibility of success**. You don't have to be sure you'll succeed; you just have to believe that success is a possible outcome in the situation.

6. Fear of success makes you anxious about what might happen if you were to become successful. You could feel in some way as if you don't deserve success. Or you might worry about success trapping you on a path that will be new and different from the one you've been on before.

To reassure this fear, you need the **belief that success is okay**—that it's good for you to get what you want in life. There's nothing wrong with becoming successful. If you truly believed that, you wouldn't be afraid of it.

7. Fear of disapproval prevents us from doing anything new, or even being noticed, because we're anxious that others might disapprove of us or of what we're doing.

Five: Finding Your Personal Fear Antidote

This fear needs **self-sufficiency**—the belief that you're capable of making your own decisions and knowing that they're the right ones for you. Remember the client I described in Lesson One who feared disapproval? She and I worked together to boost her self-sufficiency so that she could overcome this fear.

This is the approach of making friends with your fear. You find out what your fear needs to be reassured that you're going to be okay. Then, you provide for yourself more of that element. Knowing, as you now do, which fear is strongest for you, you can identify the antidote for that particular fear from the list above.

If the element or quality that I've suggested as an antidote for your primary self-promotion fear doesn't feel quite right to you, you can substitute a different quality. When you're not sure what your fear needs to feel reassured, try asking it.

Imagine that your fear is an overprotective parental figure. Turn to it and say, "Hey, fear, what do you need? What will reassure you that I'm okay without you running the show?"

You may think that some of the positive qualities I've listed as antidotes aren't all that different from one another. It may seem, for example, like confidence and self-sufficiency are a lot alike, and you might wonder why I'm identifying them as different qualities.

There are subtle differences between each of the qualities I've named. If you have confidence, for example, you might be able to put your business cards in your pocket and walk into a networking event. But without self-sufficiency, you could feel as if you don't have the right to be there, and therefore shrink away from talking to people.

Don't get too tangled up in the distinctions between each of the positive qualities. The important factor is that you pick the one quality which you feel would be the most reassuring to your fear. If it's a different quality than the one I identified as that fear's antidote, that's fine. It needs to feel right to you.

Once you have a specific reassuring quality chosen for yourself, in the next chapter, you'll explore some specific ways to build that positive quality as a path to managing fear.

How it can look to reassure your fear

The approach of making friends with your fear that I'm describing is based on the idea that instead of fighting with the fear of rejection, or trying to push down the fear of failure, or denying fear of disapproval, you'll get to know that fear and work to reassure it.

You'll identify a positive quality that will make that fear lighten up. Then, you'll determine how you can build that quality in yourself as a path to reducing the fear's power.

Here's an example of how this can work. I had a client who was having a really hard time growing his business because he was afraid to say no to anyone who wanted to work with him. He was afraid that his income would become unstable, so he took any business he could find, and was always busy on client projects.

The problem was that he ended up working with clients who couldn't pay him enough, so he was underearning. And, some of these clients asked him to work on projects that weren't really in his wheelhouse, so they took him longer to accomplish. By working with these lower-paying clients who had him working on projects that weren't the type of work he was best at, he was too busy to pursue the higher-paying, more satisfying work he really wanted.

He and I identified together that his fear was of the unknown. He didn't know what would happen if he were to turn down these undesirable projects, so he kept taking them. The answer to what would reassure that fear turned out to be knowledge, in the form of evidence.

He had a visual learning style, so I suggested that he create a chart of his earnings, plotted against the kind of projects he was working on. He created the chart, then began to experiment with what happened when he turned down a less-desirable project.

What he discovered was that the more of these projects he turned down, the more he started to earn. He had built his knowledge with evidence to counter his fear of the unknown. Whenever the fear showed up, he would look at the chart, and reassure his fear with the knowledge that refusing these projects would turn out okay.

By working to build his knowledge, he was able to manage his fear, and over time, it became less and less powerful. He would still feel a twinge of fear when he turned down a project, but armed with knowledge, he was able to say no to it, and hold out for the work he truly wanted.

When I was interviewed by Michel Neray, the developer of Purposeful Storytelling, he made the following comment about this approach:

> Michel: *It's almost like rewiring the brain, isn't it? Because the brain is wired to have a certain kind of fear reaction in the face of some certain circumstances and you're literally providing evidence to the brain that shows otherwise.*
>
> C.J: *And, it's very situation-specific. In that client's situation, he had a fear of the unknown, so we worked on building knowledge. In another client's situation, her fear was disapproval, so we worked on building self-sufficiency. That helped her fear of disapproval to not be so active.*

Skills practice: Discover your best fear antidote

Your skills practice for this chapter is to begin by taking an action that triggers your primary self-promotion fear. Depending on what that fear is, you might place a phone call to a stranger, write a follow-up email to a prospective client, go to a networking event, or publish a blog post. Notice what fear is coming up for you, and confirm that you believe this is the primary fear you should work on.

Then, imagine yourself with more of the positive quality that I've suggested above to serve as the antidote to that fear. Picture yourself as more confident, more self-assured, or more comfortable with what you're doing—whatever the appropriate antidote would be.

Present your fear with that antidote. You might just think and feel what that would be like, or, you could say it aloud, like this: "Hey, fear of the unknown, I have more knowledge now. I don't have to be afraid anymore."

Try to fully step into what it would be like for you to have more confidence, or comfort, or the belief that success is okay. How might that reduce or shift your fear?

Five: Finding Your Personal Fear Antidote

If the process of picturing yourself with more of your chosen positive quality and presenting it to your primary fear makes you feel at least a little less fearful or resistant, you've chosen a useful antidote to work on building, and you're ready to move forward to Chapter Six.

If stepping into your positive quality doesn't seem to have any impact at first, wait a day, and try again. If you still don't notice any difference, feel free to try out a different positive quality to develop instead.

You're not—yet—looking for a dramatic difference, just a subtle shift. When you've selected the best positive quality to work on developing, you'll be able to feel the possibility of a change in your level of fear.

Dale Carnegie once said:

"If you want to conquer fear, don't sit home and think about it. Go out and get busy."

That's exactly what I'm asking of you, and good advice for us all.

Six: Developing Your Fear Antidote

Manage your fear by building up its opposite

In the last chapter, you learned the strategy of making friends with your fear or resistance in order to manage it better. You examined your primary self-promotion fear to determine what that fear would need for it to be reassured.

For each of the seven likely self-promotion fears, I suggested a specific antidote—a positive quality you could build in yourself to reassure your fear. I asked you to choose one positive quality that you could work to develop.

In this chapter, you'll learn how you might build your chosen fear-reassuring quality to help you overcome your fear. You'll discover specific strategies you can use to manage fear or resistance with positive action.

As you read the sections below about each of the antidotes or qualities, pay attention to which of the quality-building strategies you think might be helpful for you to try out. At the end of this chapter, I'll be asking you to choose at least one strategy to try.

Even though you should be starting this chapter with the fear antidote you will work on already chosen, read all seven of the "Skill" sections below, not just the section that pertains to your chosen antidote. You'll find that all of the sections contain helpful ideas.

Skill: How to develop the antidote of confidence

To build confidence, one simple strategy people often say helps them greatly is positive affirmations.

A study published in the journal *Personality and Social Psychology Bulletin* showed that people perform better in high-stakes situations when they use self-affirmations to calm their nerves. Study

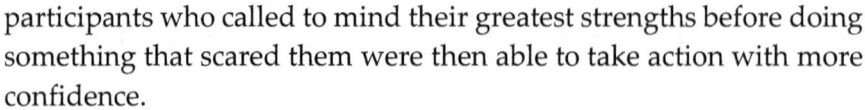
Six: Developing Your Fear Antidote

participants who called to mind their greatest strengths before doing something that scared them were then able to take action with more confidence.

> According to one of the researchers, Sonia Kang:
> *"Any time you have low expectations for your performance, you tend to sink down and meet those low expectations. Self-affirmation is a way to neutralize that threat."*

A positive affirmation is a phrase that affirms a truth you'd like to better integrate into your belief system. For example, a phrase that might help build your confidence around self-promotion could be: "I am excellent at what I do."

You can post this phrase on your computer, your refrigerator, your dashboard, or your bathroom mirror, and say it over and over again throughout the day to remind yourself of it. This will help you to reassure your fear of rejection by building your confidence.

You'll find more ideas for building confidence later in this chapter.

Skill: How to develop the antidote of self-assurance

Here's an idea about how to build the positive quality of self-assurance, an antidote for the fear of ridicule.

> Rick: *The thing that's helped me is thinking that everything I'm doing is practice for the next time. So it doesn't have to be perfect. That's a great kind of little mind thing, which is actually right. It puts me in a different frame.*
>
> Joyce: *That's a dress rehearsal.*

Dress rehearsals are a technique I've found quite helpful to build the antidote of self-assurance.

If you are going to a networking event and you'll have to introduce yourself to strangers, put on your networking clothes, fill your pocket with business cards and rehearse with the mirror. Say your self-introduction, reach out to your reflection to shake hands, and practice making eye contact. Get a kinesthetic feeling in your body of what it's like to do this thing that you're finding scary.

By rehearsing what scares you, you can become more self-assured and feel less as if there's any possibility of being ridiculed.

> According to Stanford neuroscientist Philippe Golding, who specializes in treating anxiety:
>
> *"Exposure is hands down the most successful way to deal with... fears of any sort."*

Skill: How to develop the antidote of comfort

What if you are dealing with fear of embarrassment and need to build your comfort level? Read how one of my students described herself doing that:

> TM: *What I've been practicing with my coach is my elevator speech and creating a space for me. It's really been very, very helpful. It's a safe space for me to make mistakes and trip, and know that I won't be criticized or ridiculed where those fears are. I can just do it and be it.*
>
> C.J: *That's wonderful. You actually named four separate things that you could experience in working with a coach. I want to mention the things specifically because they are things someone*

could do with a supportive friend or colleague also. The first one was role playing—have a role-playing conversation with someone. The second one was, be challenged—have someone challenge you to do your best, to be your best, to break past a barrier. The third one was being held accountable—to have someone to who you're reporting, "Okay, this is what I'm going to do... Alright, now I'm going to do it... Okay, now I did it." That accountability can also help you get past things that are barriers for you. The fourth one was having a safe place. And you didn't mention this specifically, but I think that part of having a safe place is being able to talk about what it is that you're becoming aware of with your fear and how to accept it.

Role playing in a safe place is an excellent way to go about building your comfort level.

Skill: How to develop the antidote of knowledge

When you're dealing with fear of the unknown, you need to build your knowledge. One powerful way to do that is talk to people who have already been where you need to go. Ask a friend, a colleague, or a mentor who's had some success in one of the areas where you've been feeling fearful to describe to you, step by step, what it was like for them to take that step.

For example, talk to someone who says they have gotten clients from speaking in public. Ask that person to walk you through the whole experience. What happened? What was it like? Are there any words of wisdom about it they can pass along to you?

Try to gather as much as knowledge as you can about any area where you're fearing the unknown. When you shine the beacon of knowledge into an unknown space, it lights up all the dark corners.

Skill: How to develop the antidote of belief in the possibility of success

If you're experiencing fear of failure, you need to build your belief in the possibility of success.

Read this exchange with two of my students where they make some suggestions about how to do that.

> Nancy: *Earlier we were talking about perceptions—it was suggested to me one time to go out and find your raving fans and have them give you feedback on what you do well, what your strengths are, and what appears to come easily and effortlessly to you. It really gave me a boost. It gave me reassurance that people perceive me in a much more positive way than I perceive myself when the fear kicks in.*
>
> C.J.: *That's a wonderful one, Nancy. You called them raving fans; I sometimes refer to those people as champions. To surround yourself with people who are your champions, your raving fans—that's one of the reasons that I think support groups for sales and marketing work so well. If you can regularly meet with a group of people who are really your champions, it gives you a positive sense of feedback on an activity that otherwise can give you a lot of negative experiences.*
>
> *For many people who sell their own services, you'll find that to get a sale, you probably have to go through about 29 "no"s to get each "yes." That experience of getting all those "no"s can be extremely discouraging. You can feel as if you're doing the wrong thing, that you're never going to get a client, that what you're doing isn't working, that it works for everybody else but not for you—all of those critical inner conversations.*
>
> *If you can have a group of people around you who are going through the same thing, and who are championing you by saying, "Okay, you're on 'no' number 28—just one more, and*

you're gonna land a client," that championing of you can assist in building that belief that success is possible.

What are some other suggestions for fear management strategies that you've used, you've seen used, read about, heard about?

Grace: *I think it's a great idea to keep a success log so that you begin collecting evidence that you really can do this. It's something that I've used with a number of my clients. It's so easy for people to focus on what they haven't done right. But I get them to flip it around and write down even the little things that did go their way, where they took a little risk, and it had a positive outcome.*

They begin stretching and building those muscles, and it's fun to look back later at the log, and you have a record of all of these wins. Sometimes referring to that log can help pump you up before making some scary phone calls.

C.J: *That's a great suggestion. There's a couple of variations on it that I've seen. One is the success journal, where you look at the end of every day at what went right today. What was a success? Even on days when you feel as if nothing's gone right, you force yourself to stop and look: "Okay, I'll bet something went right today. What was it?" Allow yourself only to write in your journal those things that were successful and none of the failures.*

A second variation is keeping a log of positive feedback from your clients, like testimonials that you got or thank-yous that people sent you. When you're feeling down or feeling fearful, you can pull out that collection of wonderful things that people said about you and remind yourself: "Hey, I'm really good at this, and other people think so, too."

I have found that last suggestion very helpful. Every time a client expresses appreciation to you, save a copy, or write it down, and put all those client acknowledgments in a folder.

Whenever you're worried about failure, read a few of them. Allow yourself to feel the love and appreciation those people have given you. You can override the negative litany in your head with thoughts like: "Thanks so much for all your help," or "You really saved the day," or "I don't know what I would have done without you."

Just a few minutes of steeping yourself in client love can turn your fear of failure around.

Skill: How to develop the antidote of belief that success is okay

With fear of success, to reassure that fear, you need the belief that success is okay. When success becomes scary is very often when it takes on other people's definition of it. But what's *your* definition of success? And more importantly, what's your definition of a positive view of success?

Here's what one of my students said about how he approaches that:

> David: *For me, one of the most effective ways is to reconnect to what's truly important for my life.*
>
> C.J: *How do you do the reconnecting, David?*
>
> David: *The process feels like going inside, to sense what am I doing on this planet? It's like connecting to something that calls me through the fear. It's not like I have to bust through it. There's something that's actually more important.*
>
> C.J: *That's wonderful. I think it's extremely helpful to give yourself the strength to get through this tricky, sticky place by connecting to something that has more power than that.*

Six: Developing Your Fear Antidote

> *You mentioned "the call," David. For many of us who are in the business of providing our services to others, a big part of what that's about is helping people. If we can connect to the call that brought us to this place of wanting to help others, and feel that within ourselves, instead of being focused on our own fear, we get focused on those other people outside ourselves that we want to help.*
>
> *What David is suggesting is to go inside and to ask yourself questions like: "Why am I in this business to begin with? What brought me here? What was my motivation? What's the vision for what I'm wanting to create?" And use that as a place of strength to come from.*

Visualize what the positive aspects of success are for you, and keep those in front of you. Remember who the people are that you want to help with your business, or the peace of mind you'll achieve if you have a sustainable level of income. Keep your focus there, instead of on the parts of success—as defined by others—that you fear might be unpleasant or difficult.

Skill: How to develop the antidote of self-sufficiency

The last of the seven fears I named is fear of disapproval. What that fear needs to lessen its power is self-sufficiency. If you are self-sufficient, you're able to fill your own needs without external help; you don't need the approval of others.

According to Dr. Steve Taylor, the author of *Out of the Darkness*:

"People with strong 'self-sufficiency' aren't too concerned with other people's opinions of them. Slights don't affect them so much, because they have a deep-rooted sense of their own worth."

To build your self-sufficiency, stop asking for permission from anyone in your life. Whether it's a prospective client, your significant other, colleagues, co-workers, or your family, hold on to the belief that you don't need their permission to do or say what you believe is the next right thing.

Instead, give yourself what I call a Special Permission. This is a technique I incorporated into the *Get Clients Now!* program, where I ask you to establish a permission you grant yourself each day, in order to become more successful at getting clients.

A Special Permission might sound like:

- I have permission to ask for what I want.
- I am able to try things I've never done before.
- I deserve to be well-paid for my work.
- I can make a good living and still have time for family and fun.

Craft a Special Permission that's a fit for you, and grant it to yourself at the beginning of each day, and whenever your fear of disapproval shows up.

Strategies to develop fear antidotes

The examples above describe how to build the positive qualities that will help you make friends with your fear and give it what it needs. Read the recap of these suggestions below, and think about

Six: Developing Your Fear Antidote

whether the suggested strategy feels right to you, or whether you'd prefer to substitute a different strategy to try on.

- If you need confidence, try positive affirmations.
- If you want to build your self-assurance, use dress rehearsals.
- To increase your comfort, try role playing in a safe place.
- To build your knowledge, gather information, especially from those who have gone before you.
- To boost your belief in the possibility of success, interact with one of your champions, read your fan mail, or keep a success log.
- To increase your belief that success is okay, connect with your positive vision of success and keep it in front of you.
- To build your self-sufficiency, grant yourself a Special Permission and remind yourself of it daily.

It may be that none of those suggestions on how to build the positive quality you're seeking seem quite on target for you, so below are a few more ideas you might choose from.

> *C.J: Those are all wonderful fear-management strategies that can help you with building those positive qualities. Trina, can you give us something out of NLP that would help with this? NLP, Neuro Linguistic Programming, is a discipline that has a wealth of techniques for doing a variety of reprogramming.*
>
> *Trina: There's lots of techniques. One that I'm thinking of that's very simplistic is imagining yourself in your most powerful you. So, you would see perhaps a competent, confident person.*
>
> *For example, if I was coaching someone, I would say, "So just imagine that the you that's confident has these qualities, what does that look like as you look at that you?" As they notice what they look like, they express it outwardly.*
>
> *They'll say, for example: "My body is straight. My breathing is deep. I'm noticing I'm walking down the street and I'm talking to people very easily."*
>
> *Then I would say, "Imagine what that feels like in your body, and embrace it." Then put it back on the picture again. You would practice that each day.*
>
> *C.J: That's wonderful, Trina. You imagine the powerful you and step into that, feeling the experience of it.*
>
> *Trina: It's very, very powerful.*
>
> *Vaughan: You just said something kind of interesting. I started training in martial arts again this week, so I think that might have been part of my positive shift, too.*

Six: Developing Your Fear Antidote

That's another idea for building confidence, self-assurance, or self-sufficiency—take classes in a martial art. Clients and students have reported to me that when they take martial arts classes like aikido, it gives them a physical sense in their body of being able to better take care of themselves. They become more comfortable with how their body moves, and have more of a sense of the power in their body.

By having that bodily experience, it translates into an emotional experience of how you deal with situations that you find threatening. It gives you more internal strength.

Along that same line, you can often shift into a more positive sense of self by making use of your body. Get your body in motion. Studies have shown it's hard to be depressed when you're moving.

The dialogue below has more examples.

> CJ: *What are some other suggestions?*
>
> Jim: *I go on long hikes out in nature, and when I come back, it puts everything in perspective; it makes all this seem trivial. When I get back, I feel energized and raring to go.*
>
> C.J: *Taking a walk is a time-honored method of dealing with negative thoughts. It's a great one. Get yourself out of your normal environment. If you can't take a walk, look out the window.*
>
> Michael: *I just thought of another kooky thing I've done before. I remember one time I had an interview with a company. I put on some really fast dance music and I got up and danced before I called them. It got me up, it got my juices going.*

Skills practice: Try on a strategy to develop your fear antidote

Your skills practice from this chapter is to choose just one quality-building strategy that you'd like to work with for a while.

Before moving on to Chapter Seven, take one self-promotion step that often brings up fear or resistance for you. You might schedule a networking conversation with a potential referral source, decide to write some new copy for your website, or plan to call someone you need to follow up with.

When any fear or resistance shows up, don't deny it or avoid it. Acknowledge that the feeling is there, without judging it, then employ your antidote or quality-building strategy. Say one of your positive affirmations, or interact with one of your champions, or get up and dance.

Then, notice how your fear or resistance has shifted, and see if you can move forward with the self-promotion step you chose.

Here's what it might sound like to choose one of the quality-building strategies and try it out.

TM: *I'm going to look at that aikido.*

C.J: *Great. What attracts you about that, TM?*

TM: *When I was going through soul typing, I was told that aikido would be associated with my soul type. I know that's a little bit off what you were saying, but that's what attracted me to it.*

C.J: *There's nothing off about that at all. When you look at your soul type as a way of choosing, you're looking at who you are and what would be more natural for you, and pursuing that. That's a great reason to choose, TM.*

Six: Developing Your Fear Antidote

Kris: *I'm going to keep a success journal because my biggest thing is the fear of success. It seems oxymoronic to me and yet it is there. I've done a success journal in the past, and I kind of fell off the wagon. I think it would be nice to get back on it.*

C.J: *Great idea, and I love the fact that what you've chosen to do is to reinforce the very area where the fear lies. It's a great example of going toward the fear instead of away from it, and that's so powerful.*

Martin Luther King said:

"We must build dikes of courage to hold back the flood of fear."

By choosing a positive quality to build for yourself and working to develop that antidote to fear, you will be building your own dike of courage.

Seven: Quick Fixes for Fearful Moments

Building up your fear antidotes will take time and practice

In the last chapter, you learned specific strategies for developing a fear antidote—building a positive quality in yourself that will enable you to manage your fear. I hope you tried out one of those strategies, and that it helped you lessen the negative impact of fear and resistance on your ability to promote yourself.

You may have realized that developing one of those positive qualities in yourself is not going to happen overnight; it will take time and continued practice to build it. I encourage you to make that investment of time and effort. Keep practicing the strategy you chose until you feel as if you no longer need it. I'll remind you of that recommendation at the end of this book.

But I recognize that, meanwhile, while you're building a positive quality that will ultimately lessen your fear, you need to be promoting your business *now*. You can't put it off until you feel as if you have more confidence or comfort or self-sufficiency. So, in this chapter, you'll learn some quick fixes that you can use in any fearful moment.

Please don't feel that using one of these quick fixes implies that you have some sort of injury for which you need a crutch. As I've noted before, fear is a natural human reaction to feeling at risk, and some level of self-promotion fear is perfectly normal for self-employed pros.

In fact, in a survey of 2,000 entrepreneurs, when they were asked about the biggest obstacle to making their first sale, more people named fear than lack of money, lack of knowledge, or lack of time.

Instead of considering these quick fixes to be crutches, think of them as training wheels. While you're learning to ride the cycle of fear management, you may need to put on some training wheels to help you along.

In this chapter, you'll discover five different quick fixes for fear and resistance that will help you promote yourself despite any negative feelings you may be experiencing.

Skill: Become a problem-solver

For many of us who market our own services, we get all tangled up in resistance to doing anything that reminds us of our unpleasant associations with selling. You don't want to brag; you don't want to have to convince people; you don't want to take steps that feel manipulative.

Good for you. You don't have to do any of those things in order to market your business.

The first quick fix to help you overcome that type of resistance is to think of yourself as a problem-solver instead of a salesperson. In selling situations, ask questions about what your prospective clients need. Then, suggest solutions for their needs, whether or not those solutions involve you and your services.

Act as a resource to help potential clients get what they need. Instead of worrying, "How do I get this sale closed," make your primary focus, "How do I get this person's problem solved?"

When you take on the persona of problem-solver, instead of thinking what you're doing is selling, it puts you into the role of being helpful to the person you're talking to. That's a much more comfortable role than the salesperson role, which sometimes feels like you're trying to convince someone to do something that they don't want to do. Working hard to convince a reluctant buyer is typically not a happy experience for you or for your prospective client.

Instead, let your role be to listen to what's going on with your potential clients, and to suggest what might help their situation, even if that suggestion doesn't involve hiring you. Stepping into this role can shift the way that you think about what you're doing. Taking on this helper role can make you much less fearful and lead you into territory where you don't have as much resistance. It can also allow you to be much more upbeat and positive when you speak to a potential client.

The dialogue below provides an example of how this can work.

> **Kenneth:** *I don't have too much problem getting booked into a presentation. My issue is the next day after the presentation when it's time to follow up. Where I get stopped is I start thinking about me being the person who gets called for follow-up, and how much I hate those calls. Now I'm going to be doing the very call that I dislike. So, I don't do them.*
>
> **Stephanie:** *Can I offer a suggestion on that? I will try and look for something that I can use for the follow-up call that would be helpful to them, that's completely separate from what I want to sell, and say, "I just wanted to give you a call and give you this information (this website, this whatever, something else that we had talked about), because I thought it would be really helpful for you. And, oh, by the way, have you had a chance to look over that... blah blah blah?"*
>
> **C.J:** *I think Stephanie's suggestion is really good. It's a great way to think about "How can I contribute value in this conversation?" instead of having the conversation just be about getting a sale.*
>
> *There's also a step past that which can be helpful, which is to imagine—before you place a follow-up call—how much value you're going to contribute to this person's life once they hire you. To really visualize if you were to solve this guy's problem, this is what it would create for him. If you were able to provide this solution for that woman, this is how her life would be different.*

Seven: Quick Fixes for Fearful Moments

Then make the call from that place, knowing that if they don't work with you, things are not going to be as good for them. And, this conversation is the necessary place to get them from that stage where they are, where things are not so good, to a place where things are really working well.

For a lot of people that can get you over that hump of feeling like, "Maybe I'm bugging that person," when you call.

Kenneth: *That's good!*

One thing you do have to look out for with this approach is that you need to know at what point you should ask someone to become a paying client. You don't want to give away everything you'd like them to pay you for. But, it can be much less scary for you to ask for their business if you're already starting to give them something.

Sometimes that transition between being generous and asking to get paid can feel a bit uncomfortable. Here's a way to approach it. Let's say you're in a networking situation where you're in conversation with someone. You've been giving that person some free advice and you realize that they would benefit by hiring you.

You might make a statement I first heard as a suggestion from a psychotherapist who had often found himself listening to people's troubles at cocktail parties: "Perhaps you should engage me in my professional capacity."

You can even be a bit light-hearted about how you say this. It will help the person you're talking to realize that you've been giving them valuable advice, so they can make the shift to thinking about becoming your client.

That's the first quick fix. Consider how might you be able to help your prospective clients now, before they even hire you. Shifting into being a problem-solver will let you act in a way that is probably right in the center of your comfort zone.

Skill: Talk about your clients

The second quick fix is to tell stories about your clients instead of talking about yourself. When a prospective client asks, "How can you help me?" answer by saying, "Let me tell you about a client of mine and what her experience was." Then tell a story about what happened for that client while she was working with you.

Begin by describing the situation the client was in when your work began. Include what problems the client needed to solve, or what goals the client wanted to achieve.

Continue by describing what you did to help that client. Be as specific as you can, while maintaining appropriate confidentiality. Tell the story of the steps you took to get the client what they needed.

Wrap up your story by recounting the results your client achieved because of your work. Mention any tangible outcomes for the client like decreased expenses or a new job, as well as intangible factors like increased optimism or less conflict.

You can make this approach even more powerful by preparing in advance two or three client stories that illustrate typical projects or engagements for you. Then practice telling the stories aloud.

See the guide "Telling a Client Success Story" in the Appendix for more suggestions and an example.

With a storytelling approach, you don't have to brag or talk yourself up. All you do is simply describe the experience someone else had when they worked with you. As a result of this, the person you're talking to can get a feel for who you are, how you work, and how what you do helps your clients. The story you tell can be all about the client, with none of it centered on you.

For most self-employed pros, you can have a much less fear-provoking sales conversation when you talk about clients instead of about yourself.

Skill: Be yourself, not a salesperson

The third quick fix is to forget about trying to act like a salesperson and be authentically yourself. It's so easy to forget in the selling process that your strongest place to stand is the place where you naturally are.

Selling is such an artificial, awkward situation for many, because it's not your natural way of operating in the world. But if you can remember to relax into being yourself, you can be much more effective at closing sales.

Read this dialogue between me and Michel Neray of Purposeful Storytelling.

> C.J: *Assume that the actual content of your elevator speech is in place, that you know what it is that you want to say. But, the problem is being able to say it confidently, at the right times, instead of feeling like, "This is stupid," or, "I shouldn't brag about myself."*
>
> *What's necessary are two different things. One is to recognize that the people you're going to be saying this to are people who you're trying to help. They're people who you are trying to be of service to. If they don't know that you have this thing to offer, then they're not going to get that help. They're going to be out there lost and struggling because you weren't able to voice to them how you can be of service.*
>
> *Stepping into that mindset can take away a lot of the initial fear of verbalizing, "This is what I do and this is what I can do for you."*
>
> *The second piece is to look for the way to say it that feels completely authentic and connected with the way that you want to present yourself to the world. All of us have different flavors, and if you're a chocolate person, you can't go about promoting yourself as a strawberry person.*

Michel: *I'm so glad to hear you say that, C.J. You hit one of my biggest pet peeves. When I hear so-called gurus giving the quote-unquote formula, I just cringe when I hear that, because the formula that may work for one person may not be at all the right formula for somebody else, and I think that's what you're saying.*

C.J: *Yes, the way in which you talk about what you do needs to be in alignment with who you are and how you want people to think of you.*

One of the mistakes that we make is to step into this sales and marketing persona. We feel like in order to get the business, we need to somehow become someone different than who we are when we're actually delivering service to our client after we've gotten the business. That's the worst possible thing to do.

If you find yourself taking on a sales and marketing persona — that selling voice, that marketing stance of tensing up and inhaling and gritting your teeth and going, "Okay, I've gotta do it" — that's absolutely the wrong direction.

What you want to do is relax, release, get grounded in who you are, and talk to people authentically. That's what's going to enable you to make the connection that ultimately leads to getting the business, and also is going to enable you to get past any fear you have about what you're about to say.

Now, what does being authentic actually sound like? Of course, it will be different for everyone, but this dialogue will give you an example.

C.J: *What Lalita said was that getting presentations — landing sales conversations — was the place where she was feeling stuck. When you uncover something like that, the question you want to ask yourself is: "Now that I know that, what might be creating or causing that to be the case?"*

Seven: Quick Fixes for Fearful Moments

Lalita: *Some of the things that I'm concerned about in the very beginning part of the sales process is being appropriate and not appearing manipulative. I'm bending over backwards to be appropriate with people, and that may have me listening for cues that aren't there, or that tell me to back off.*

C.J: *It sounds like something that's getting into the mix is some hesitation that you have about moving forward because of how it might appear. Not wanting to appear manipulative, not wanting to be too pushy, perhaps?*

Lalita: *Yeah.*

C.J: *If you were to make up what might be a solution to that, any ideas?*

Lalita: *Umm, I could ask people how they want this piece of the process to go, tell people what I'm concerned about, that I am concerned about being appropriate with them? I don't know.*

C.J: *I love both of those answers because where they come from is a very authentic place. One of the spots where we get hung up in selling is that we put on our sales face and we try to behave like we think salespeople are supposed to behave.*

Lalita: *Flip it around for me, I'm trying so hard not to be. I just despise how I see people selling to me. So, I'm turning my skin inside out trying not to be that.*

C.J: *What I want to point out, though, is that is your sales face. You see what I'm saying? Not like you're pretending to be a salesperson like those salespeople you don't like. What you're doing is you're putting on a face in order to avoid being that, and that is your sales face.*

We've all got our own. It's different for all of us. For some people, we try and put ourselves into the pushy salesperson place, because we think that's the way we're supposed to do it.

For others of us, we're trying to avoid being too aggressive, too pushy, so instead what we do is we back off.

What you were suggesting a couple of minutes ago was something which is a marvelous sales approach, which is being completely authentic about it. Even saying something like:

"This is the part of the conversation that gets kind of awkward for me, because what I want to do is I want to tell you all the reasons why I think this would really help you, and I feel like that might be too pushy, and you might think I'm trying to persuade you to do something you don't want to do. Tell me, how would you like this part of the conversation to go?"

That's what I mean by being really authentic. For you, it sounds like that's an approach that could be very helpful.

Jim: *That's worth the price of admission right there.*

Skill: Find a less scary path

The fourth quick fix is an approach to get moving again when you feel immobilized by fear and resistance. Use the I AAM technique from Chapter One to identify the specific fear that has you stopped, then look for what else you might do that doesn't provoke that fear.

This conversation about in-person networking will show you an example.

Rick: *I guess what I notice is that almost all of them I don't like. Almost all of the things that are listed in your "Networking that Works" bullet points, I don't like doing. So, I need to think of different ways, or translate them differently so they fit with me. Like more one-on-one, personal things that work better for me, instead of feeling like I'm on display, or I have to go "be the show" or something like that.*

Seven: Quick Fixes for Fearful Moments

C.J: *You know, I personally don't like mixers. The stand-around-with-a-drink-in-your-hand-talk-to-people-at-random format.*

Rick: *Right, I hate that.*

C.J: *Some people like it; they thrive in it. To me, it's not a comfortable environment. What I've noticed is more comfortable to me is go to a mixer where there are display tables available, and stand behind one of those tables to talk to people. That's comfortable, because now I've got a job to do. So, if I'm in an environment where there isn't some formal structure like that, I will often create one for myself.*

I'll show up at an event where I don't know anybody, and I'll introduce myself to the organizer and ask if they need any help. That immediately gives me a job to do, and that's where I step into doing what I do best, which is having a job to do and doing it well. That's a great role for me, and because I know that, and I function really well there, it's a perfect way for me to network.

Rick: *So, when you do that, it's like whoever you're talking to informally, the conversations develop naturally. Is that what you're saying?*

C.J: *Absolutely, conversations develop naturally.*

Vaughan: *I have a comment about that. If you want to go to a professional society meeting or whatever, it's always a good idea to be fifteen minutes early, because that gives you an opportunity to make contact with the speaker and to help the people set up. Never arrive on time; always get there early.*

C.J: *It's a very good tip, Vaughan. And, even if you do something as simple as finding out where the coats go and the bathrooms are, it makes you invaluable to the event, because now, all of a sudden, you know the answer to two of the most commonly asked questions.*

Vaughan: *And, the key people remember you as one of the people who helped them make it a success.*

C.J: *Yes, they do. You can stand near the door even if you don't have an official role, and help people out as they come in. "Hi, the hors d'oeuvres are over here and the desserts are over there." People look at your name tag, and what happens next is very often a conversation.*

Because these people coming in, they're lost, too. They want somebody to talk to. If they don't know anybody else there, they're so thrilled to see a friendly face. By the time you leave the event, you'll have met dozens of people that otherwise it might have been awkward for you to connect with.

That's an example of looking for where you already know you can find your personal—not just comfort level, because sometimes it is uncomfortable to push yourself a little bit beyond what you normally might do—but a place where you're functional. Where you know you can do a good job instead of where you might get immobilized.

There were two examples in the dialogue above of finding another path to take when you feel stopped by something. My two students felt stopped by the idea of going to a networking mixer. Rick suggested having one-on-one networking conversations instead. Vaughan and I talked about how you could go to the event but give yourself a job to do instead of standing around wondering how to start conversations.

The key to this approach is to ask yourself, whenever you feel stuck or stopped by fear or resistance, "What else can I do?" You'll be surprised to discover that very often, you have an answer to that question.

Skill: Play a different tune

The fifth and last quick fix I suggest is that you play a different tune. I mean that quite literally. Remember how Michael described in a dialogue in Chapter Six that he put on some fast music and got up to dance before he had to place a challenging phone call? Or, my suggestion in Chapter Two that you set your self-introduction to music to serve as your theme song?

In studies published in the *Journal of Positive Psychology* and the *World Journal of Psychiatry*, researchers found that listening to upbeat music can improve not only your mood, but your self-esteem and self-confidence.

Psychologists and brain researchers tell us that music naturally evokes and engages our emotions. Just listening to music can increase the amount of dopamine and serotonin produced in your brain.

The happiness hormone, oxytocin, has been shown to be released by singing, regardless of whether you can carry a tune. Playing an instrument, or improvising on one, will give you a boost. Even chanting or drumming have similar positive effects. And of course, dancing to the music will engage your body also.

Think about what songs or style of music make you feel upbeat, positive, or more powerful. You might choose something like Michael Franti's "Say Hey," Queen's "We Will Rock You," "Happy" by Pharrell Williams, Beethoven's "Ninth Symphony," known as the "Ode to Joy," or "Walking on Sunshine" by Katrina and the Waves.

Using music to shift your mood can work very quickly, and can change how you feel about the next step in front of you, from the inside out.

Skills practice: Continue building your fear antidote and add a quick fix

As your skills practice for Chapter Seven, continue practicing the strategy you chose earlier for building a positive quality to lessen your fear. Just like before, intentionally take a self-promotion step that often brings up fear or resistance for you. Acknowledge that the negative feeling is there, then employ your quality-building strategy. After doing that, notice how your fear or resistance has shifted, and see if you can move forward with your intended self-promotion step.

Here's the new piece to add to your practice. Choose a moment when fear or resistance has you stopped. It may be after you've already tried your fear antidote, and the fear has shifted, but not quite enough for you to be able to move forward. Or, it may be an entirely different occasion.

Either way, find a time when you realize that you're stuck about some type of self-promotion and you want to get past it. Then try one of the five quick fixes I suggested:

1. Become a problem-solver.
2. Talk about your clients.
3. Be yourself, not a salesperson.
4. Find a less scary path.
5. Play a different tune.

Make sure you practice both of those elements before moving on to Chapter Eight—practice your quality-building strategy, *and* try out a quick fix.

....

Rosa Parks once said:

"Knowing what must be done does away with fear."

....

By having a quick fix in your back pocket, you will always know what you can do next, and begin to gain power over the fear that's been holding you back.

Eight: Defeating Fear with Stronger Relationships

Overcoming fear at a deeper level

In the last chapter, you learned five quick fixes for diminishing your fear and resistance quickly. I asked you to try out one of those quick fixes to see how well it worked for you. I also suggested that you continue to practice one of the longer-term strategies I've suggested for building your positive qualities in order to make friends with your fear.

The fear management approaches you've been learning so far—employing the I AAM Technique, exploring the Practice Loop, managing your inner critic, identifying your primary fear, working to build the positive qualities that will reduce fear for you, and making use of quick fixes to handle fear in the moment—will absolutely make a difference in your ability to manage fear and resistance around marketing and selling.

If you continue to use those approaches, you'll see powerful shifts in your mindset and the results you're able to produce. And, in this chapter, I'm inviting you to take your fear-busting work to a deeper level, to provoke an even more profound change. Here's how that can happen.

According to numerous studies over the past two decades, positive social support helps us humans to build resilience to fear and other types of stress. When you have strong relationships with other people, groups, and the larger community, you're better able to cope with all kinds of adversity.

A study published by the journal *Psychological Trauma* found that social support helps people better manage fear and anxiety, even when their condition is as severe as post-traumatic stress disorder.

There are two ways that forming stronger relationships with others can help you overcome fear. One approach is to build

Eight: Defeating Fear with Stronger Relationships

relationships with other self-employed professionals and creatives who are dealing with challenges similar to your own. You'll find more about that approach later in this chapter. The other approach is to build stronger relationships with the people you want as clients.

A huge part of successful marketing and sales is about relating to people, which happens to be something that many self-employed pros are quite good at. When you create a solid relationship with a prospective customer, marketing and selling becomes much easier.

If you believe you aren't good at forming new relationships, you may be surprised to discover that learning to market and sell can actually make you better at them. It works both ways—getting better at creating relationships will improve your marketing, and getting better at marketing will improve your ability to form relationships. If that doesn't make sense now, it may begin to by the time you finish this chapter.

It's easy to forget when you're caught up in the selling process that you're interacting with other human beings. Sales and marketing endeavors can feel like artificial, awkward activities, because they aren't your natural way of interacting.

But the person on the other end of your phone call or email, or across the table from you, or reading your web copy, is someone just like you, with their own goals and dreams and intentions. The more connected you can get to whatever those goals and dreams and intentions are, the more effective you become at marketing and selling.

The flip side of this truth is that one of the surest ways to shoot yourself in the foot as a marketer or salesperson is to get out of relationship with the people you are marketing to by turning them into adversaries.

Unfortunately, that's a model of sales and marketing we've all seen—salespeople trying to pressure a customer into making a purchase with aggressive techniques, manipulative language, or even outright deception. But that's not who you are, and it's definitely not who you need to become in order to sell and market.

Instead of treating a prospective client as an adversary, you want to both be on the same side. That's how you're going to win their trust, and therefore win the sale. To truly be on the same side as your client, you need to get to know them.

Here's an example of how it can work to place your focus on building relationships instead of on making sales.

A client of mine was dealing with a great deal of fear and anxiety about marketing himself as an IT consultant. He'd tried to have his own business several years before, and failed at it. This time around, he wanted to make a go of it, but he was afraid of another failure.

His fear made him afraid to pursue a sale, even after he'd identified a prospective client. The answer he found to this dilemma came from a surprising place.

My client had two pre-teen children, a boy and a girl, who were active in school sports. They both swam and played soccer competitively. Attending swim meets and soccer matches for both the boys' and girls' teams, my client was always standing by the sidelines with other professionals who were also parents.

I asked him if they ever talked about work, and when he said no, I suggested he bring it up as a topic of conversation. He wouldn't do any promotion or selling; he would simply get to know these other parents more fully instead of talking only about kids and sports and school.

Within a month, my client had one signed contract, a second promise of business later in the year, and an introduction to an exec at a company he had been wanting as a client for ages. All from using the time he was already spending at his children's competitions to get better acquainted with other parents.

Skill: Building relationships with prospective clients

The type of relationship-building I described above is something we humans naturally do—we get to know each other while engaged in an activity of mutual interest to us.

This is why in-person events designed for people to network can be so successful as a way to meet new people. Everyone at the event has chosen to participate in the same activity. Instead of an interaction like a sales call, where the only agenda is for one person to sell to another, you're both doing something else, and while that's going on, you have a conversation.

The most common settings we think of to meet potential clients are business or professional meetings like networking mixers, association gatherings, or conferences, but these are by far not the only possibilities. You can begin building relationships with prospective clients or potential referral sources in your local area by going where they already are. (There's more below about people who aren't local.)

The people you'd like to meet could be:

- Taking a class or workshop
- On the commuter bus or train
- Waiting in line at the coffee shop or takeout spot
- Attending a social function, like a wedding or housewarming
- At the gym or yoga studio
- Living on your block
- Volunteering for the same cause
- Attending worship services
- Going to a school or after-school activity
- Participating in a hobby or sport
- Seeing a concert or play

I got to know one of my best clients because we both do various kinds of handcrafts. We originally met at a neighborhood garage sale, looking through a pile of crafting supplies, then got to know each other better by participating in crafting afternoons organized by the woman who held the garage sale.

I've met others who became clients, students, and referral sources at classes I've attended, at social events, volunteering, and through my weekly writing group.

If events designed specifically for networking aren't your thing, you don't have to attend them. Humans have been doing what we now call networking for millennia without the benefit of official networking events.

Meeting someone in person in one of the ways above is how a relationship can begin. All you need to do when you meet someone new is remember this: ask what that person does for a living, and tell them what you do. If it seems like there could be a connection, the next step is to build the relationship you just started.

If the venue where you met is a place where you will meet again, the start of the relationship is often simply going back to the same place multiple times, and making it a point to talk again with people you met before.

When you meet in a setting where you may not see each other again, express interest in further interaction, and ask for the person's contact information. If your exchange was pleasant, most people will give it to you without hesitation. Then look for a next step in getting to know each other better.

Can you invite them to coffee or lunch?

Are there other local events that might be of interest to you both, like a seminar or professional meeting? Let them know you're planning to attend an upcoming event, and ask if you might connect with them there.

Is there a social or sporting activity that you like to engage in which you could invite them to share with you? Depending on your interests and theirs, this could be a sports match like a ball game; a community event, like a fundraiser; a cultural event, such as a concert; or even just a walk in the park.

For the people you'd like to get to know better who aren't local, or are maybe too busy to make time for meeting in person, you can still build relationships with them.

You can talk to them on the phone or by video chat—not as a sales call, but as a get-acquainted conversation. You can send them notes with links to, or copies of, items in the news that you think will be of interest. You can connect with them on social media, and interact with what they post.

You can create content in your area of expertise like blog posts, articles, a white paper or case study, or videos, and reach out to let them know these items have been published. You can host a virtual event, like a webinar, video conference, live chat, or Ask Me Anything session so they can get to know you better in company with others.

All of these are valid ways of building relationships with people who could become your clients and referral sources.

The last group of relationship-building ideas I listed—social media, producing and sharing content, and virtual events—are also approaches you can use with prospective clients when the service or product you want to sell them is too low-cost for you to spend one-on-one time with each person.

How can you meet people in the first place when they aren't in your local are? One of the best ways is through referral sources—people who you've built relationships with previously. You can also meet people online through social media, taking virtual classes, giving virtual classes, virtual volunteering, and online communities.

Transcending barriers to relationship-building

You'll find that some people will be open to these relationship-building contacts and some people won't. But you won't find that out until you offer. I suggest that you consider the possibility of giving yourself permission to not pursue as clients those people who aren't interested in building a relationship. Instead, pursue only the ones who are.

It's just like how you become friends with people. When someone is open to friendship, you move closer to that person; you take steps that reflect the growing friendship. When someone isn't open to friendship, you usually don't push it very hard. You might extend a few invitations and when you don't get a positive response, you stop trying and move on.

But, if you keep trying to make friends, you do get them. Because there are people out there who *are* interested in having a relationship with you.

By devoting your efforts to building relationships only with those people who are open to it, you can have positive results that feel much more comfortable than trying to push yourself on the people who don't respond well.

What you're doing with this relationship-building approach is treating your prospective clients as if they were your colleagues, or even your friends.

When you do this consistently, it's very common to have business come to you as a natural result. And often, that kind of business will be much more satisfying for you than business you must struggle to get.

For many self-employed pros, this is a way of moving forward to build your business without necessarily triggering your fears of self-promotion at all.

Let me interject that I do understand introversion and shyness. I'm an introvert myself, and I can be shy around people I don't know. This is why it's so important to look for activities and environments that feel natural to you.

If it feels like too much of a stretch to invite someone you don't know well to have lunch, then make it a group lunch where you also invite a colleague or two you're already comfortable with. If talking on the phone isn't your favorite way to communicate, then make good use of email.

Keep looking for which relationship-building activities feel the most natural to you, and you'll find approaches that will work.

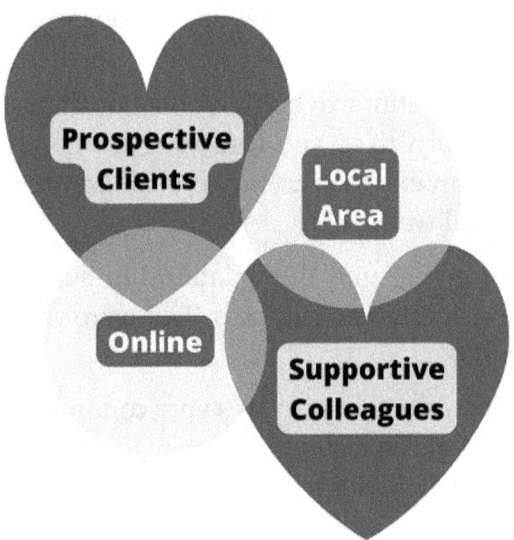

Skill: Building relationships with supportive colleagues

I mentioned above that there's another group it's worthwhile to build relationships with, in addition to potential clients. You will also benefit by building relationships with other self-employed pros and entrepreneurs.

Several times throughout this book, I've suggested you might get help from a colleague—situations like practicing your self-introduction, role-playing a selling situation, or having someone join you for lunch with a prospective client. To take advantage of these ideas, you need a pool of supportive colleagues to draw from.

Interacting with colleagues can also help you normalize what you're experiencing. You'll hear from others that they, too, have self-promotion fears. You'll learn that you're far from the only one who encounters setbacks in trying to get clients, which can make you feel much better about yourself and your efforts.

If you don't know many other business owners, consider how you can meet some. Are there professional or community meetings in your local area that other self-employed pros attend?

Check out resources like Meetup.com, your local Chamber of Commerce, or your local small business development center or entrepreneurship center for ideas and event listings.

Attending seminars and workshops on small business or industry topics can be another good way to connect with new colleagues. Search for them on Eventbrite, Facebook events, or LinkedIn events, as well as within your professional associations.

When your local area doesn't offer many opportunities to meet other entrepreneurs, or you have limitations that prevent you from getting out, look online for communities that host conversations on topics that might be appropriate.

You'll find groups on Facebook or LinkedIn, Discord communities, discussion groups, message boards, and mastermind groups, where you can gather virtually with others like yourself. Your professional associations may host some of these, also.

Once you meet some other business owners in a live or online setting, choose one or two at a time that you'd like to develop further as colleagues, and reach out with some of the relationship-building approaches I suggested above.

Over time, you can build up a group of peers you can rely on to provide both tactical and emotional support as you continue your journey of learning to manage self-promotion fears.

You'll find that the more you focus on building natural relationships, the less fear you'll have around marketing and selling overall.

Skills practice: Begin to build more relationships

Your skills practice exercise for this chapter is to identify three people you already know: one prospective client, one potential referral source, and one self-employed colleague.

For each one of these people, identify one relationship-building move you can make, and take a step to get it started. For example, you could:

- Invite them to coffee or lunch.
- Find a local or online event that might be of interest to you both, let them know you're planning to attend, and ask if you might connect with them there.
- Identify a social, cultural, or sporting activity that you like to engage in, and invite them to share it with you.
- Schedule a phone call or video chat, not as a sales call, but as a get-acquainted conversation.
- Send them a note with a link to, or copy of, a news item that you think will be of interest.
- Connect with them on social media, and interact with one of their posts.
- If you have content you've created like blog posts, articles, a white paper or case study, or videos, reach out to let them know about a recently published item.
- If you host a virtual event, like a webinar, video conference, live chat, or Ask Me Anything session, extend a personal invitation to them.

Then, consider the ideas I've suggested in this chapter for meeting new people, and pick one of those approaches you'd like to use on a regular basis, starting now.

Once you meet a new person, in any setting, consider whether that person could be a client, a referral source, or a colleague for you. And if so, decide what relationship-building step you will take to begin the process of getting to know your new contact better.

In the concluding section that follows, What to Do When You Finish This Book, you'll find an ongoing program for you to continue employing all the strategies you've learned throughout the book, so you can carry on learning to manage fear and resistance into the future.

Erica Jong declared:

"I have not ceased being fearful, but I have ceased to let fear control me."

That's exactly what you are becoming able to do.

What to Do When You Finish this Book

Put it all together and take it on the road

To continue employing all the strategies you've learned throughout this book, and build on your skills for managing fear and resistance, put all the techniques together, using these six steps.

Step One

From now on, every time you notice that you are holding back on any self-promotion activity, use the I AAM technique from Chapter One. Notice what fear or resistance or inner critic conversation is happening. Accept that you have that feeling or thought without judging it. Remind yourself that you can move ahead regardless.

Step Two

Next, see if the Practice Loop can help you move forward. Can you prepare how you want to be and what you need to do to take the next needed step? Can you then practice it, notice how that went, and incorporate what you noticed when you take the step for real?

Step Three

After that, if you're still feeling challenged, and you believe it's your inner critic in the way, use the three steps you learned to manage the critic: Notice what the inner critic is saying. Respond by disputing what the critic says. Debrief the results and try to move forward again.

Step Four

If it's fear rather than the inner critic—or in addition to the critic—that's holding you back, identify it as one of the seven fears you learned about.

Step Five

Get into alliance with your fear, remembering that it's trying to protect you from harm. Recall to yourself the positive quality you chose to build in yourself to reassure that fear, and see if you can call that quality forth in the moment.

Step Six

If you're still feeling stopped, use one of the quick fixes from Chapter Seven to get past your fear right away, so you can take the step necessary to keep building your business.

These six steps are what you should follow every time fear or the inner critic has you stuck or stopped. If you employ these approaches consistently, over time, you'll be able to transform your relationship with fear from "False Evidence Appearing Real" to "Face Everything And Recover."

Keep on building relationships and your fear antidote

There are two other practices I suggest you adopt as ongoing activities to continue strengthening your self-promotion muscles.

First, continue to build relationships with both potential clients and supportive colleagues. Make relationship-building a regular part of your business activities. Consider blocking out time on your calendar each week for this specific purpose, and scheduling coffee, phone calls, excursions, or whatever your chosen paths are for building relationships.

The more people you get to know in your marketplace and field, the easier and less fearful self-promotion will become.

Second, keep working to build the positive quality in yourself that you identified as your best fear antidote. Use one of the strategies you learned in Chapter Six, such as role-playing, keeping a success log, or reminding yourself of your Special Permission.

Make your antidote-building activity a daily practice, not something you do only when you think you need it. If a particular practice starts to lose its juice for you, choose another practice to adopt next. Keep on doing this for as long as you keep experiencing any sort of self-promotion fears.

And if *that* turns out to be for as long as you're self-employed, congratulations! You will have joined the ranks of business owners who have a daily success practice that keeps them motivated and inspired to do the challenging work of getting clients.

To set an intention for how you plan to continue the work of overcoming your fear, consider creating a written fear management plan you can refer to in the weeks to come. See "Sample Fear Management Plan" in the Appendix for an example.

> One of my favorite quotes about fear comes from author Louisa May Alcott:
>
> **"I am not afraid of storms, for I am learning how to sail my ship."**

That is my hope for you—that you will continue to sail on, fearlessly, to your desired destination.

Appendix

Crafting a Self-Introduction That Gets Noticed

Self-introduction. Elevator speech. Ten-second introduction. Thirty-second commercial. Whatever you call it, you need one to be an effective marketer, salesperson, or even jobseeker. Here are six keys to creating one that produces the results you are seeking.

1. There's a difference between a 10-second introduction (self-introduction) and a 30-second commercial (elevator speech). By my definition, the 10-second intro is a concise summary of what you do that can be used when you shake someone's hand, stand up to introduce yourself briefly to a group, or call someone on the phone.

In the formula I use for composing intros—the benefits-oriented introduction—it contains just one key benefit to get people's attention, plus a simple title or label for what you do. (There's more about this below.)

A 30-second commercial, on the other hand, shares more about what you do, who you do it for, the products and services you offer, and/or your competitive advantage. You might use this when leaving your first voice mail message with a prospective client or referral source, introducing yourself as a speaker, at a leads or networking group where this longer format is expected, or to lead off a sales presentation.

I find it useful for most entrepreneurs and salespeople to have both forms of introduction handy.

2. Your introduction should be composed with generating referrals in mind, not just on attracting any clients who might be present. It's more important in my view to have an intro that a 12-year-old could understand and repeat than to have one that pinpoints your specialty to someone in the know. You are statistically much more likely to be speaking to a potential referral source than a prospective client at any particular moment.

Even better is to have two 10-second intros in your pocket—one that you use when you don't know who you're speaking to, and one that you use when speaking to someone who you already know understands your specialty.

3. In the benefits-oriented introduction formula, you lead with a key benefit and statement of who your clients are, then provide a label or title that identifies your profession. If your listener won't have a chance to ask you questions about what you do immediately after hearing your intro, including all three pieces of information will help people remember and "file" you appropriately, whether it's to refer you a client or hire you themselves.

Here are some examples:

- "My name is Peter Marconi and I provide Chicago financial services firms with persuasive tools for winning new clients. I'm a marketing communications consultant."
- "I'm Carmen Sanchez, and I help working mothers take practical steps toward living a more fulfilling and balanced life. I'm a life coach."
- "I'm Fred Patel, and I deliver talented, high-caliber professionals to fill essential positions at information technology companies nationwide. I'm an executive recruiter."

4. Keep in mind that your introduction will not always be used in interactive situations. If you are shaking someone's hand or speaking with them live on the phone, you can use an intro that is intended to provoke curiosity or questions. But if you are using your intro to stand up and introduce yourself to a group (networking meeting, leads group, etc.), or to begin a letter, email, or voice mail message, it's more effective to develop an intro that gives the listener a category to "file" you under.

For an example of how this works, imagine you are currently in the market for someone to create a logo and business cards for you. Person A leaves you a voice mail message that says, "My name is Angela and I help people like you get more clients. Please call me."

Person B leaves you a message that says, "My name is Sam and I help small businesses get noticed. I'm a graphic designer."

My bet is that even though neither of them mentioned logos or business cards specifically, you would be likely to call Sam back and not Angela. I would also bet that if you heard both Angela and Sam introduce themselves at a networking group, and you had no need for their services but the next day someone asked you to recommend someone to create their new business card, you might remember Sam from his intro, but wouldn't think of Angela.

This type of mental "filing" by category is how most people's brains work. If you're crafting an intro for use in this type of one-way communication, I'd recommend including your own filing label.

5. In the benefits-oriented format, you state a key benefit of your services (and if possible, your target market) before naming your profession. There are two reasons for including a benefit like this and for saying it first. The first purpose is to position you in the minds of your listeners as you would like to be positioned, before they make up their own minds about you.

If you simply say you are a graphic designer, business attorney, or communications consultant, without giving your listeners any other details, they categorize you as they please. But if you also name a benefit you provide your clients, they can determine much more about whether they or someone they know might be able to use you.

The second reason is to make your introduction memorable. This is why you might choose to make your benefit sound almost like a tagline. If you go to a networking event and meet three different accountants there, you are much more likely to remember the one who said something clever or relevant than the others who simply told you what they do for a living.

Years ago, I would regularly run into an accountant at local events who always introduced herself this way: "My name is Cathy Cheung, and I love taxes! I'm a CPA. Call me at tax time, and I'll help you save money." I probably haven't seen Cathy in 20 years now, but I still remember her.

6. Whatever you choose to say should sound and feel authentic when coming from you. If you are a naturally enthusiastic, high energy, or humorous person, superlatives and catchy phrases can be quite appropriate. If you are understated, conservative, or serious, your introduction should reflect that instead.

There's a whole spectrum of personalities between those two extremes, of course. My point is that there's no one right "flavor" for an intro that suits everyone. If your introduction authentically represents who and how you are, and it turns some people off, those people probably aren't good clients for you.

The authenticity of your self-introduction is more important than pleasing all possible listeners. If you feel comfortable saying it, and it attracts the kind of clients you want, then you've found the right formula.

Telling a Client Success Story

When interacting with potential clients and referral sources, a helpful self-promotion tool is a collection of client success stories. Everyone loves to hear stories—we find them entertaining, educational, or evocative of deeper emotions. We identify with people through the stories they tell.

Client success stories are tales of moments in your business when you overcame challenges to help your client succeed. Telling these stories creates a memorable impression and gives the listener anecdotes about you that they can repeat to others. Your stories can help your contacts make the connection between the problems or opportunities of their situation and the person (you) who can provide a solution.

Here are three steps to creating a client success story:

1. Setup — What was the situation? Describing the client's pre-existing situation, problem, or opportunity sets up the plot of your story. Example: "I had a client... contract... job... situation... who/where..."

2. Action — What did you do about it? You may have developed plans, assigned tasks, held meetings, written proposals, or implemented a hands-on solution. Describe the methods you used to tackle the situation, mapping out the process in detail, all the way through to resolution.

Use active, descriptive verbs to illustrate what you did. Examples: "So I analyzed... evaluated... diagnosed... assessed... clarified... reviewed... collected... compiled... solved... advised... recommended... influenced... negotiated... persuaded... planned... drafted... authored... formulated... adapted... designed... composed... created... invented... engineered... constructed... built... developed... installed... set up... purchased... integrated... produced... prepared... performed... implemented... supervised... coordinated... facilitated... trained... taught... coached... managed... directed... arranged... organized... executed..."

Appendix

3. Payoff — What happened as a result? Explain the positive end result. Be specific about the increase, change, or improvement that resulted from your actions. If there was a measurable impact of your work, value it in dollars, percent of change, or another quantifiable factor. If the result was less tangible, describe it in qualitative terms like increased satisfaction, reduced pain, or improved outlook.

Examples: "And as a result, my client achieved... attained... resolved... determined... retained... restored... raised... increased... reduced... earned... gained... won... expanded... strengthened... improved... enhanced... fixed... corrected... succeeded... conquered... pioneered... transformed..."

Here's what a completed client success story sounds like:

"I had a client with a human resource system that was absurdly complex and hopelessly out-of-date. It had been modified in-house by an employee who was no longer there, and was being operated by a technician and a data entry clerk who hadn't been adequately trained. In addition, there was almost no documentation of how to use the system.

"I assessed the situation and began to reverse engineer the programming code to discover how the system worked. In the first 30 days, I was able to produce ample documentation to run the system error-free on a daily basis, and I trained the technician and data entry clerk sufficiently for them to work with minimal supervision.

"Then I prepared an evaluation of the system, and recommended that it be completely replaced. After my recommendation was accepted, I joined an inter-departmental team dedicated to evaluating and selecting a replacement system, and later joined the system replacement team. There I served as the expert on duplicating needed functionality from the old system, and managed data mapping and conversion.

"As a result of my work, my client was able to replace their outdated and error-prone HR system with a new system that completely met their needs, while at the same time keeping their old system fully operational. The whole project took only 18 months from the day I was first hired, and was completed on time and within budget."

Sample participant's fear management plan

"I plan to use the six steps for fear management each time I find myself fearful or resistant about self-promotion, paying particular attention to disputing my inner critic, 'The Schoolmarm,' and overcoming my fear of disapproval. I'm going to spend four hours per month working on building relationships with potential clients and my colleagues. And, I'm going to continue building my fear antidote of self-sufficiency by granting myself a special permission at the beginning of every work day."

About the Author

C.J. Hayden is a business coach, writing mentor, and the author of seven other books, including the bestselling *Get Clients Now! A 28-Day Marketing Program for Professionals, Consultants and Coaches*. The *Get Clients Now!* book is now in its third edition, and has been translated into multiple languages. Thousands of self-employed professionals and creatives around the world have made *Get Clients Now!* their sales and marketing bible.

Since 1992, C.J. has coached and trained self-employed professionals to get clients, get strategic, and get their writing done. She has over 40 years of business management experience, holds the credential Certified Professional Co-Active Coach, and completed advanced coach training with the Coaches Training Institute and Arbinger Institute.

In addition to her books, C.J. has written hundreds of blog posts and articles on marketing, entrepreneurship, and nonfiction writing. She hosts monthly Get It Written Days and an online community for self-employed professionals and creatives who write.

A popular speaker and workshop leader, C.J. has presented hundreds of programs to international audiences, and taught classes for John F. Kennedy University, Mills College, and the U.S. Small Business Administration.

To find out more about C.J.'s books and programs, or to schedule an interview, visit cjhayden.com.

Are you a coach, counselor, or trainer who would like to lead programs based on this book? Please check out my book the *Facilitator's Guide to Overcoming the Fear of Self-Promotion.*

Did you find this book valuable? Your brief review will help spread the word. Please take a moment to leave a review with your favorite bookseller or review site. Thank you! I appreciate your support.

www.ingramcontent.com/pod-product-compliance
Lightning Source LLC
Chambersburg PA
CBHW071709040426
42446CB00011B/1988